Divine
ARISE

STEP OUT OF HIDING AND
EMBRACE YOUR SACRED VISIBILITY

TIA BREWER-FOOTMAN

ISBN: 979-8998830303

Produced by Publish Pros | publishpros.com

DEDICATION

To the daughters of Zion—called, yet hidden. This is for every woman who wondered if her light was still needed. May this ignite what Heaven planted in you. Arise, for your time is now.

To my hubby, my Boaz and bestie—thank you for covering me with love, joy, and quiet strength.

To my mommy, my first mentor and sunshine—your resilience lit the path I now help others walk.

And to Father God, my Pappa—thank You for eyes to see, depths to sense, and the high and low places where You prune me for greater works.

TABLE OF CONTENTS

The Pace of Grace: Trading Hustle for Heaven's Rhythm

Let There Be Legacy

Crowned for Influence

A MESSAGE
FROM THE AUTHOR

Dear Divine One,

Welcome, beloved. Whether you stumbled upon this book or prayed your way here, trust that your arrival is not random—it's divine. This isn't just reading material; it's a gentle summons from Heaven. You've been invited into a sacred conversation where identity, healing, and destiny meet.

Divine Arise was never meant to rush you into performance or pressure. It was written to help you move at Heaven's pace—slow enough to hear, soft enough to be shaped, and strong enough to obey. As you journey through these pages, you'll uncover the spiritual gifts God breathed into you before time began and learn to walk in the grace that's already yours.

The message of this book was born from Isaiah 60–61—the prophetic invitation to arise and shine, for your light has come (NKJV). It is a declaration of glory after seasons of exile and silence, a reminder that God's mercy still finds us in the dark and calls us into His marvelous light. And while Isaiah gives us the why of arising, Psalm 119:105 gives us the how:

"Your word is a lamp to my feet and a light to my path."

That verse has become my compass. It reminds me that divine direction rarely comes in floodlights—only in lamps. We move forward one illuminated step at a time.

Throughout the book, you'll notice Sacred Exercises and Sacred Prayers woven into the chapters. Think of them as invitations, not instructions. You're not expected to complete them all; instead, follow the leading of the Holy Spirit. Choose what speaks to your spirit in the moment. Some sections and chapters hold several, others only a few—and that's intentional. Each one meets you in a different season of becoming.

When you see a prompt to pause to pray, grab your journal, or make note, treat it as a small doorway—an intimate pause where Heaven bends low to meet you. Take your time. Listen. Let what you write and pray become part of your personal dialogue with God.

And as you begin, set an expectation. Be honest about what you hope to gain—clarity, confirmation, or perhaps the courage to rise again. God delights in that kind of honesty.

As a former news journalist turned Kingdom reformist, I used to report the facts; now I reveal the Truth. I came from man-made lights, but I'm here to point you back to the Light—the One who sees, heals, and sends. Whatever brought you to this moment, know this: You are not here to simply read a book; you are here to remember who you've always been.

Let's arise together.

With love and grace,

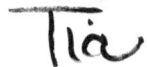

INTRODUCTION

KINGDOM ALLEGIANCE

A Divine Declaration for Sacred Sisters of the King

Before you go further, let's make it official. This isn't just a book—it's a divine summons. You're stepping onto sacred ground where identity, power, and purpose collide.

If you feel that stirring—deep calling unto deep—and you're ready for real, this pledge is your anchor. A royal reintroduction to who you are, why you're here, and how Heaven intends to move through you.

Repeat aloud:

> I rise today as a daughter of the King—
> I pledge allegiance to the Kingdom of God
> And to the blood of Jesus—my covering and command.
> I am His ambassador, part of the ecclesia—
> Deployed to occupy until Earth reflects Heaven.
> I walk by the Spirit, not the flesh,

Led by His Word and established in His truth.
I take territory in my assigned metron.
And as His government rests on His shoulders—
Now, through Christ, that authority rests on me.
I govern as He governs—
through justice, righteousness, and peace without end.
In Jesus' name, Amen.

The Word
That Builds

CHAPTER 1

IN THE BEGINNING, THE WORD

Before there was social (media) or a stage, there was a Word. In the silent void before creation, before any structure, the voice of God declared, "Let there be light," and light burst forth. In the beginning, God's Word initiated everything—it was the first cause, the genesis moment for all that is. And in the Gospel of John we read, "In the beginning was the Word, and the Word was with God, and the Word was God." This tells us that at the very origin of all things stands the eternal Logos (Word). For us as daughters of God birthing new dreams, this is a gentle, profound reminder: Our true beginning must also be His Word.

Picture the Holy Spirit hovering over the formless deep at creation—nothing visible yet, no platform or product, only God's presence and promise. Creation didn't emerge from hustle or human design; it began when God spoke. In the same way, before you sketch out a business plan or launch a ministry, you need a word from the Lord. The Word is our genesis. It carries creative power. When God breathes a word over your life, that word contains the blueprint for fulfillment. Our role is not to invent the vision, but to incline our ear and receive it.

I've lived this firsthand.

I remember a time when my husband and I were stretched thin, juggling high-level consulting projects for major beauty and health brands—campaigns with L'Oréal's ethnic division, Soft Sheen Carson and Mizani, initiatives tied to Disney, and even a gospel-centered event in partnership with McDonald's. Every opportunity was significant, but we were spiritually and mentally overloaded. We needed clarity—urgently.

That's when we entered into the Saint Paul Fast, inspired by *The 9 Supernatural Fasts for Breakthrough* by Dr. Elmer Towns. As we fasted and prayed for direction and the removal of any spiritual scales, God gave us undeniable clarity. That fast helped us confidently close one chapter and look ahead with peace about where He was leading us next.

It impacted us so deeply that I began recommending the book to others so they could experience the same kind of freedom and focus. I even wrote to Dr. Towns to share our testimony. He responded with such humility, and we had the sweetest exchange. That moment solidified the power of fasting as a divine tool for clarity—not just for us, but for others called to move boldly in purpose.

Sometimes, receiving the Word doesn't come from a cloud-parting moment. It comes through consecration. Through clearing the clutter and seeking Heaven's voice with intention. The Word that builds is not rushed—it's revealed.

Even Jesus Himself is called "the Word made flesh"—the living Logos who dwelt among us. The Word is a person, alive and active. When you anchor your work in Christ, you're building on the immovable Rock. Heaven's assignments always begin with Heaven's word. We don't start by scrambling for ideas; we start by sitting at His feet and listening.

The sacred pattern continues throughout Scripture. Before Abraham could become the father of many nations, he first received a word: "Go from your country, your people and your father's household to the land I will show you" (Genesis 12:1). Before Moses could lead an exodus, he encountered the Word in a burning bush. Before David could slay Goliath, he carried a word of covenant identity and divine protection in his heart. Each one had to first receive before they could achieve.

HEARING HEAVEN'S WORD

Before you take your next big step or build your next big thing, you must first hear Heaven. Consider Ezekiel, who was commanded to eat the scroll before prophesying (Ezekiel 3:1–3). The Word had to be consumed—internalized and digested—before it could be proclaimed. This sacred principle still applies: what we build must begin in the secret place where Heaven speaks and our spirits receive.

Now pause for a moment. Close your eyes and ask the Holy Spirit:

>   » What word are You speaking over my life in this season?

>   » Is there a Scripture that contains the blueprint for my next step?

» Lord, what are You saying about the vision I'm carrying?

Write down what you hear—even if it's just a phrase or a single Scripture reference. Date it. Return to it often. This becomes your sacred starting point.

CHAPTER 2

HEAVEN'S ASSIGNMENT VS. HUMAN AMBITION

There is a profound difference between human-driven ambition and a heaven-breathed assignment. Ambition compels us to chase trends or personal fame, but a Word from God calls us to build something eternal. Ambition has us laboring to make a name for ourselves; a divine assignment has us laboring to exalt His name. One brings anxiety, the other brings peace.

As the late Dr. Myles Munroe—a renowned pastor, leadership expert, and teacher on purpose—once taught, success in God's Kingdom is measured not by the size of our platform but by how well we fulfill His purpose for us. The greatest tragedy is to be successful at something God never told you to do. True success is completing the specific mission He's given you. When we grasp this, we stop striving to do *everything* and start focusing on the *one thing* Heaven has entrusted to us.

Aligning with God's assignment requires surrender. Sometimes He asks us to lay down a seemingly good idea because it didn't originate from Him. Yet God's "no" to our human designs is really a "yes" to something greater He has in mind. Remember Abraham and Sarah: They were ambitious to force God's promise by conceiving Ishmael, but the true assignment—Isaac—came in God's miraculous timing.

Consider King Saul versus King David. Both were anointed, but Saul's ambition led him to overstep his boundaries, offering sacrifices that weren't his to give (1 Samuel 13:8-14). His impatience cost him the kingdom. David, however, refused to take the throne by force. He waited for God's timing because he understood that position without divine permission is just ambition, not assignment.

Their stories make one thing clear: Not every open door is from God. Which is why we need discernment.

HOW TO DISCERN ASSIGNMENT FROM AMBITION

While the two may look similar on the outside, assignment and ambition flow from two different spirits. Here's a framework to help you discern the difference:

- **It aligns with Scripture and God's character.**
  God will never call you to do something that contradicts His Word.

- **It persists through seasons.**
  Divine assignments have staying power. They aren't driven by market trends or fleeting excitement.

- **It requires faith beyond your natural ability.**
  If you can do it without God, it's probably not from God.

- **It serves others and advances His Kingdom.**
  Heavenly assignments lift others up. They don't just amplify your personal brand.

- **It brings deep peace, even amid challenge.**
  You may feel stretched, but not frantic. Assignment carries grace.

- **It's confirmed by godly counsel and divine affirmation.**
  When God speaks, He often sends confirmation.

- **It produces life, not burnout.**
  It leads to freedom, not striving. Joy, not torment.

Before you chase the next big idea, come before the Father. Let Him search your heart. Because if it's born of the Spirit, it will bear the fruit of the Spirit. But if it's born of the flesh, it will eventually drain you.

SACRED PRAYER | *Father, I surrender every ambition that originated from my flesh or others' expectations. Show me what You have written on my scroll before the foundation of the world. I choose Your assignment over prestige, ease, or worldly validation. Purify my motives and align my heart with Your perfect will. In Jesus' name, amen.*

CHAPTER 3

THE LOGOS BEFORE THE LOGO

In our modern marketplace, it's easy to get caught up in branding—logos, taglines, aesthetics. But the Holy Spirit gently reminds us the Logos (the Word) comes before the logo. Your message precedes your marketing. God's voice establishes your value long before any brand does.

Think of Mary of Bethany, who sat at Jesus' feet when others were busy. She chose the "better part"—the Word Himself—and Jesus said it would not be taken away from her. Mary's "brand" wasn't one of hustle, but of devotion. And yet her influence endures wherever the gospel is preached.

When the Word takes root in you, your "brand" will naturally reflect Heaven's design. You won't have to force an image, because you'll radiate His image. The logos you carry internally will shape the logo you present externally. Start with the Word at the center, and everything else—mission statements, visuals, offerings—will flow in proper order and impact.

Consider Saint Francis of Assisi, a 13th-century monk and reformer known for his radical devotion to Christ, heard God's clear instruction to "rebuild My church." Francis initially thought God meant the physical structure of San Damiano, but soon realized the Lord was calling him to spiritual renewal. His movement of radical simplicity transformed the medieval church precisely because he stayed true to the word he had received. His "brand" of barefoot poverty and joyful worship was birthed, and he flowed from the logos, not clever marketing.

Or look at William Wilberforce, an eighteenth century British parliamentarian and devout Christian whose decades-long fight against slavery stemmed from a profound encounter with God's Word about human dignity and justice. Before launching his political campaign, he had received a clear logos—God's heart for the oppressed—which sustained him through years of opposition. The logos preceded and informed all his public actions.

Organizations that attempt to create a logo before receiving a logos often find themselves constantly rebranding, restructuring, and reimagining their purpose, because they built on shifting sand rather than solid rock.

THE LOGOS-TO-LOGO DEVELOPMENT PATH

When you begin to discern what Heaven is speaking, that revelation will naturally move through a development process. I call this the Logos-to-Logo Path. It unfolds in six phases, and each one matters.

It begins with the Receiving Phase, where you slow down, get quiet, and make space to hear what God is actually saying. Then comes the Incubation Phase, when you allow that word to take root in your spirit without rushing it forward. Next, the Confirmation Phase invites you to bring the word into the light—checking it against Scripture and sharing it with trusted, Spirit-filled counsel. In the Clarification Phase, the fog begins to lift and you gain deeper insight through prayer and reflection.

Then comes the Expression Phase, where you begin to articulate the word clearly and put language around the vision you've been carrying. Finally, the Manifestation Phase brings it into form: visuals, structures, and strategies emerge that reflect the word you received from God—not your personal ambition or trend-driven urgency.

THE LOGOS AUDIT

Not everything that sounds spiritual is aligned with the Logos—God's revealed Word. Sometimes we build visions based on opinions, affirmations, or trauma rather than Truth. Before branding, launching, or scaling anything, you need to audit the source. What are you building on? What are you building for?

Here are a few audit questions to help you examine your spiritual foundation:

- Is your idea rooted in Scripture or is it shaped by culture?

- Did the instruction come through prayer or did it come through pressure?

- Is the motivation to glorify God or to prove something to others?

- Will this assignment bear eternal fruit or temporary applause?

As you reflect, ask the Holy Spirit to highlight any areas where your motives or directions have drifted. Write down what needs to re-align with the Word.

CHAPTER 4

THE WORD:
YOUR BLUEPRINT AND COMPASS

God's Word is not only our beginning; it is our blueprint and our compass. As a blueprint, the Scriptures sketch the architecture of our calling. We find patterns and principles within its pages—how God calls, how He equips, how He requires obedience and molds character. Every story in the Bible is like a beam in the structure of our understanding. These are not just stories; they are construction plans for kingdom builders.

I'll never forget the first time I heard God's voice. It wasn't audible — not in the way I expected. It was a deep inner witness, one I could have easily missed if I hadn't finally slowed down. I had spent so much time serving in church that I rarely sat still long enough to receive. But one day, I sensed the Spirit prompting me to selah. Just a few quiet moments sitting—no tasks, no role—opened the way. In the stillness, I sensed the Lord speaking from within: "You've been looking for the pattern, but I'm causing you to be the blueprint."

If I hadn't sat down, I would have missed it.

At first, I thought I was losing it. Was I really sensing something from God? Was it just me? I remember turning to a few of my church sisters and asking if they had heard anything unusual. Their kind smiles and blank stares told me everything I needed to know: this was a divine revelation, just for me, in that moment.

As a compass, the Word keeps you on course when countless voices give advice. "Your word is a lamp to my feet and a light to my path" (Psalm 119:105). It shows us the next step when we can't see the whole road. Stay in the Word, and you won't stray into dead ends or detours that waste time.

In Proverbs 3:5-6, Solomon tells us to "Trust in the Lord with all your heart and lean not on your own understanding; in all your ways submit to him, and he will make your paths straight." This is the promise of divine guidance. When we align our decision-making with God's Word, He makes our path clear. Not always easy, but clear.

The Word does more than inform us; it forms us. It shapes our thoughts, transforms our values, and aligns our desires with God's heart. Through regular immersion in Scripture, you begin to think more like Christ and make decisions that align with His kingdom values.

Think of the Israelites in the wilderness, guided by God's word daily—a pillar of cloud by day and fire by night. The Lord is eager to give you daily direction as well. He may not reveal every detail of your five-year plan, but He will give enough light for today's step. Obey that, and He'll illuminate the next.

BIBLICAL PATTERN:
WORD-GUIDED BUILDERS

Throughout Scripture, we see remarkable examples of those who built according to God's specific instruction.

- ✓ Noah built the ark "according to all that God commanded him" (Genesis 6:22).

- ✓ Moses constructed the tabernacle precisely as God showed him on the mountain (Exodus 25:40).

- ✓ Solomon built the temple according to the plans David received from God (1 Chronicles 28:19).

- ✓ Nehemiah rebuilt Jerusalem's walls with the king's permission, but God's protection and direction (Nehemiah 2:18).

- ✓ Paul laid foundations according to the grace God gave him (1 Corinthians 3:10).

Each builder received specific instructions, followed them faithfully, and saw God's presence manifest in what they built. Now it's your turn to build with the Word.

STRATEGIC WORD MAPPING

Once you've clarified the spiritual origin of your vision, it's time to map the specific words, Scriptures, and instructions that will anchor your next steps. Strategic word mapping is a spiritual discipline I enjoy using. It helps you remember what God said and steward it well.

Return to your Bible, journal, and prayer time. Begin listing out phrases, Scriptures, confirmations, and impressions that have repeated across this season. Notice the patterns. Look for words or ideas that keep surfacing. Pay attention to timing, tone, and target. These are prophetic clues.

Once you've gathered this insight, ask yourself: What is God emphasizing now? Which words carry weight for this season of building?

This exercise will transform Scripture from general advice to specific blueprint material for your unique situation.

CHAPTER 5

AT THE ALTAR BEFORE
THE MARKETPLACE

Divine sister, there is an altar within you—a sacred place of devotion—and that altar must come before any marketplace impact. God often calls us to an altar experience before a platform experience. Why? Because the altar purifies our intentions and fuels us with holy fire. Only then are we ready to effectively step into the marketplace or ministry world carrying His presence.

There is profound power in beginning your day (and every new endeavor) at the altar of prayer and worship. It's where you lay down self and take up His strength. Consider Elijah: Before confronting false prophets on Mount Carmel (a very public, marketplace-like showdown), he repaired the altar of the Lord that was broken down. He restored worship in a private act before calling down fire in a public act.

Build the altar first, and the outcomes—the fire of God—will follow.

When you seek God at the altar, you are reminded why you do what you do. It's here you recall that your business or ministry exists to glorify Him and love others, not to exalt yourself. The altar puri-fies your intentions and rekindles your passion with holy fire. Then, when you go out into the marketplace, you carry the fragrance of Christ—something unmistakable and attractive to those around you.

The altar-first principle is woven throughout Scripture. Before Abraham could receive the covenant promise, he built an altar (Genesis 12:7). Before Israel could enter the Promised Land, Joshua built an altar to the Lord (Joshua 8:30). Before David could rule ef-fectively, he established worship in Jerusalem (2 Samuel 6). The pattern is evident: altar precedes advancement.

Time spent in God's presence—in prayer, worship, and meditation on Scripture—is not a distraction from your work; it is the foun-dation of your work. When you build an altar of devotion in your life, God sends His fire upon your offering. This fire purifies your motives, consumes what is not of Him, and releases supernatural power for your assignment.

FROM HIDDEN INTERCESSION TO GLOBAL IMPACT

In the 1700s, a small group of persecuted believers gathered on the estate of Count Zinzendorf in Herrnhut, Germany. Instead of immediately launching outward-focused ministries, they estab-lished what became known as the *"Hundred-Year Prayer Meeting,"* a continuous intercession that lasted over a century. From this al-tar of prayer emerged the first large-scale Protestant missionary movement, eventually sending thousands of missionaries world-wide. Their pattern was clear: they built the altar before the mission field.

This rhythm repeated itself through the ages. The Welsh Revival, sparked by young Evan Roberts praying "Bend me, O Lord," broke out with widespread repentance and a return to holiness.

Then came Azusa Street—a catalytic revival born through weeks of intercession in a humble home in Los Angeles, led by a Black holiness preacher named William J. Seymour. Under his leadership, the meetings erupted in spontaneous worship, racial unity, miracles, and the outpouring of tongues. The *glory fell where prayer dwelled.*

That revival didn't just shift atmospheres—it birthed movements. Denominations like the Church of God in Christ (COGIC), the Assemblies of God (which initially licensed its early white ministers through COGIC), and the Pentecostal Assemblies of the World (PAW) all trace their roots back to the flames of Azusa.

Bishop Charles H. Mason attended those meetings and encountered what would become his *upper room experience.* Though already rooted in holiness tradition, it was at Azusa that he received the baptism of the Holy Spirit with the evidence of speaking in tongues. That encounter lit a fire that followed him back South and laid the foundation for what became the Church of God in Christ (COGIC)—now the largest Black Pentecostal denomination in the world.

Another branch that grew from that altar was the Pentecostal Assemblies of the World (PAW), a historically Black-led Oneness

Pentecostal fellowship. Though the doctrinal distinctions varied, the spiritual roots remained the same—Azusa's fire lit them all.

Azusa proved this: the altar can birth movements. And for many Black believers, it affirmed that revival leadership and Holy Spirit power were not limited by race, status, or formal training. The Spirit fell on *all flesh*, just as Joel prophesied.

THE SACRED SPACE I DIDN'T EXPECT

As for me, I wasn't born on the church pew, which meant I had a lot to learn about the ways of God and discerning religion over relationship. Marrying into a family raised in the church (my husband was practically birthed there!) meant I was on a fast track to catching up.

I remember overhearing a conversation with Mother Footman. She was talking about the "prayer closet," and the way she described it made it sound so powerful, so sacred, so deep. I couldn't wait to get home and experience it for myself.

I marched right into our place, opened up my actual closet, stepped into that cluster of shoes, hangers, and boxes and waited for the heavens to open.

Let me tell you—there were no fireworks. No goosebumps. No tongues, no tears, no wind of the Spirit. Just me, sitting there, realizing how badly I needed to clean my closet.

And oddly enough ... that was the beginning.

Years later, I built a real prayer room—a sacred space just for soaking, for silence, for divine intel. And while I've since made every part of our home an altar to the Lord, that secret place remains my sanctuary.

Looking back, I'm actually grateful I eavesdropped on that conversation. Because what I overheard that day? It lit a fire I didn't know I needed. And now, I truly cannot live without my secret place.

That fire from the secret place eventually ignited a fresh rhythm in how I led. I remember when I first started consulting about spiritual gifts and strategy. At the time, I was running my business full force, fully aware I held the title of CEO—Chief Executive Officer.

But it didn't take long for me to realize something vital: While I was the CEO in the natural, I desperately needed direction from Heaven to truly lead. My personal prayer time wasn't enough; I needed set-apart time to meet with the One who is, and always will be, my SEO—Sovereign Executive Officer.

Years ago, I received the revelation to begin having "SEO Days." Once a month, usually on a Friday, I'd carve out this special day—a time of consecration and fasting. No client calls. No grind. Just me and the Lord.

And in those consecrated spaces, I'd receive such powerful insight. Sometimes, the strategy came like fire. Other times, the instruction was gentle: rest, take a nap, pause, Selah. Each month, the flow was different, but the direction was always divine.

Those SEO Days became my rhythm, my reset. They anchored me. They gave me prophetic clarity for the weeks ahead and helped me re-enter the business not just with plans, but with presence.

Because of those days, I became a better CEO—not just managing tasks, but stewarding a vision Heaven trusted me to carry.

That kind of clarity doesn't come by accident—it comes by altar.

SUSTAINING THE FIRE IN SACRED WORK

By now, you've seen how the altar shapes everything—your intimacy with God, your clarity in calling, and your ability to show up with power and presence. Whether you're launching a ministry, building a brand, or leading in your church or community, one thing remains true:

The secret place fuels the sacred work.

You don't need another checklist—you need rhythms that keep the fire burning.

Here are a few altar-aligned habits that help you stay connected as you build:

- **Start with God**: Give Him your first moments, not your leftovers.

- **Stay rooted in presence**: Whether it's quiet worship at your desk or pausing for prayer before big decisions, let God lead the room.

- **Honor the increase**: Dedicate your firstfruits—your income, your insights, your breakthroughs—as an offering of gratitude.

- **Check for drift**: Revisit the original instructions. Are you still aligned with what He showed you at the altar?

You don't have to do it all at once. Just choose one rhythm to re-anchor you this week.

Because when worship leads, the work doesn't have to strive. It flows.

SACRED PRAYER | *I declare that the Word of God is the foundation of everything I build. I choose the altar before the marketplace, intimacy before influence, and Heaven's voice before human validation. As I wait on the Lord and build according to His pattern, He will establish the work of my hands. What I build will stand because it is birthed by His Word, fueled by His presence, and aligned with His purpose. I arise today as a builder whose blueprint comes from Heaven, whose strength comes from worship, and whose impact carries the fragrance of Christ. Amen.*

CHAPTER 6

BECOMING BEFORE BUILDING

I didn't build anything worth carrying until the Word built me first.

Or you could be saying, "Tia, I built the altar. My prayer life and devotional time is strong." And yet, you may still feel like you've been wandering a wilderness with blueprints in hand, pouring your strength into projects that just won't prosper. You've fasted, prayed, strategized, yet doors stay closed. Could it be that the Lord, in His mercy, has been building you before allowing you to build it? Like a wise architect, He lays a deep foundation in the builder before He lays the foundation for the dream.

The Scriptures show us a clear pattern: becoming precedes building. Trying to rush ahead and construct our vision without letting God construct our character leads to collapse. Our talents may open a door, but only our character will keep us in the room. God would rather the work take longer and the worker be stronger.

Consider the construction metaphors God uses in spiritual formation. He calls us clay while He is the potter; we are shaped in His hands (Isaiah 64:8). We are living stones being built into a spiritual house (1 Peter 2:5). A house can't stand if its stones are weak. Thus, He fortifies the stones (that's us!) through pressure, heat, and time so that when arranged together, they can uphold something glorious.

Moses spent forty years in the Midian desert as a humble shepherd before he could lead a nation. In that wilderness, God stripped away Moses' impulsive anger and self-reliance and built in him meekness and obedience. Only then was he fit to construct the tabernacle and govern Israel.

The life of Joseph provides another powerful illustration. Before Joseph could govern Egypt, God had to develop his character through betrayal, false accusation, and imprisonment. What appeared to be setbacks were actually divine setups. In the pit and the prison, Joseph's character was refined. He learned forgiveness, stewardship, and faithfulness in obscurity. When the moment came for him to step into leadership, he was internally prepared because God had been working on him for thirteen years.

King David followed a similar path. After his anointing by Samuel, he spent years running from Saul, hiding in caves, and leading a band of distressed men. These years weren't wasted, they were workshops where David learned leadership, developed intimacy with God, and processed his own weaknesses. When he finally took the throne, he had been shaped by God's hand through trials and testing.

This scenario with David? It feels like home.

I was born to lead, and for over a decade, I did just that as an award-winning television news anchor for ABC, CBS, and FOX affiliates. Every morning, I woke up a quarter million viewers through my show. State lawmakers dubbed me "The Media Darling," and I made history as one of the first media personalities in my region to receive days named in my honor, keys to cities—the works.

My final station was the undisputed news leader in the market with the highest ratings. And while I held a rare dual role as both education reporter and morning anchor (a full plate that was far from typical), our co-anchored show pushed the station to even greater heights.

When I transitioned out of TV, it was completely on my terms. I still remember network agents urging me to consider national opportunities, but I felt a different pull—one I couldn't ignore. I stepped into entrepreneurship alongside my husband. There was undeniable demand for my voice, and I was already drafting a highly requested book. All signs, it seemed, were pointing to global impact.

I truly believed Daddy (aka our Heavenly Father) was launching me to the nations.

Only for Him ... to pull me all the way back.

Not into a major market, not onto a national stage—but into the quiet, unseen role of a pastor's wife. A role I didn't ask for, didn't feel equipped for, and didn't know how to carry. No armor that fit. No circle that knew how to pray me through.

And slowly, I sank. Into the cave. Into depression. I wasn't going to the nations. I was going to the corner.

Moncks Corner, to be exact—the small section of town where our sweet, humble ministry was planted.

Now listen—I don't despise small beginnings. Not at all. I was born and raised in deep rural Georgia. But I wasn't prepared for the many flavors of humble pie Daddy would have me taste in this hidden place.

It felt like I had gone from high-powered platforms to folding chairs and fellowship dinners. From ratings and recognition to navigating church hurt and culture shock. From spotlight to spiritual formation.

And yet, it was in that quiet corner—not in a newsroom or green room—where God stripped, healed, recalibrated, and redefined me.

I thought I was being benched. But He was building me.

Not for fame — but for faithfulness.
Not for applause — but for authority.
Not to perform — but to carry out something set apart.

And wouldn't you know it? From this very corner, Daddy's sending me to the nations with a different mantle altogether.

The pattern is unmistakable: God invests heavily in the preparation of the vessel before pouring out the fullness of the assignment.

WHAT HEAVEN OFTEN BUILDS FIRST

These are some of the recurring ways God refines Kingdom builders before release. You may see your current season reflected in one or more of them:

1. Integrity Testing: seasons where your commitment to truth is challenged

2. Obscurity Training: periods where faithfulness must be maintained without recognition

3. Relationship Refinement: difficult people and situations that develop your love and patience

4. Authority Alignment: learning to submit to authority before wielding it

5. Identity Anchoring: pressure that forces you to find your worth in God alone

6. Resilience Building: setbacks that develop spiritual and emotional toughness

7. Gifting Maturation: opportunities to practice your gifts in smaller contexts

Beloved, recognize that delays are not denials. God is not withholding your assignment; He is preparing you to steward it well. When you've been properly formed, you'll build with wisdom that only experience with God can provide.

SELAH MOMENT: REFLECTION FOR THE JOURNEY

If you feel led, pause here and ask:

- What character fruit is God ripening in me through this season?

- Are there unseen muscles He's strengthening right now?

- What might He be protecting me from by delaying certain doors?

As a former journalist, I've seen it all and interviewed some of the greatest, including world leaders, celebrities, and political giants. I know what's out there. God is more interested in making you a vessel of honor than He is in you being a platform of influence. If He has you in a hidden season, do not despise it. Embrace the inner work. Let the Word heal you, shape you, anchor you. In due time, you will emerge and build something lasting because it's built upon the integrity and faith forged in you.

If this season has been stretching you more than launching you, this prayer is for you. I invite you to read it slowly—line by line—letting the Spirit do the work beneath your words.

SACRED PRAYER | *Heavenly Father, I surrender to Your process. I acknowledge Your work in me precedes Your work through me. Shape me into a vessel worthy of the calling You've determined for me. Refine my character, purify my motives, and* *strengthen my faith through every test and trial. I choose to embrace the wilderness as Your workshop, knowing that what You're building in me will sustain what You build through me. In Jesus' name, amen.*

Be encouraged that you stand in good company: Every great woman of faith has had her wilderness, her hidden years, her nights of wrestling. It's not punishment; it's preparation. The Father disciplines those He loves (Hebrews 12:6) and refines those He plans to use mightily.

And do not shortcut the process. The sooner you yield to it, the sooner you're truly ready. And when the fullness of time comes, what emerges from your life will be pure, powerful, and unshakable.

CHAPTER 7

DIVINE SILENCE ≠ ABSENCE

Even when God whispers, He's still speaking.

In the hush of an unseen corner, a seed breaks open beneath the soil. No one hears it; no one applauds it. In the deep of a womb or the stillness of a cocoon, transformation begins without fanfare. Divine silence is not divine absence. In the quiet, the Word that was sown in you is alive and at work, whispering life into your very bones. You feel only stillness, even loneliness, but Heaven is humming with purpose on your behalf. In these silent seasons, God's voice may be a whisper, yet it thunders in promise: "I will never leave you nor forsake you." The silence is a sanctuary. The hiddenness is an incubation for glory.

During one of my many deep moments of revelation—the kind that helped me not only appreciate but truly recognize the value of Daddy's divine silence—I found myself in tears, heavy-hearted, tucked away in my cave. I was on the run emotionally, like David.

And that's when I sensed Papa's nudge deep in my spirit: "Come. Look out the window."

It was during the pandemic—a time when life had already begun slowing down—but that day, something felt different. I walked over to the bedroom window and peered out.

Just months before, the housing development near our home had been buzzing with life. Construction crews, tractors, and heavy machinery had filled the streets. But now, it all sat completely still. Abandoned. Silent. It looked like a deserted war zone.

In that moment, I was instantly transported. I didn't just see empty dirt and frozen equipment—I saw dry bones. Just like Ezekiel did.

And I heard the Lord ask, just as He did in the valley: "Can these dry bones live?"

Of course, He already knew the answer. What He needed was for me to open my mouth again. Then He said, "You shall speak, daughter. Otherwise, how will they hear and be encouraged? How can these dry bones live if your voice doesn't activate them? How can you nurture if you don't rise as the spiritual mother I've called you to be? And let's be clear—you are not a stepmother."

That last phrase caught me off guard. I hadn't realized I was acting timid, cautious, unsure of my authority. Having grown up in a blended family and later stepping into the first lady role behind a matriarch who'd held her seat for nearly fifty years, I subconsciously assumed the posture of a stepmother: present, but not primary, loving, but not leading. God had to correct me. I wasn't called to babysit a legacy—I was called to midwife one.

That moment changed everything.

Throughout Scripture, we see God working powerfully in silence. For four hundred years, between Malachi and Matthew, Heaven seemed silent—no prophetic word, no angelic visitations recorded. Yet during this period, God was masterfully arranging history: establishing the common Greek language that would later spread the gospel, developing Roman roads that would carry apostles, and preserving the Jewish people and their scriptures. What seemed like divine absence was actually divine preparation.

For thirty years, Jesus lived in obscurity in Nazareth. The Gospel writers give us almost no information about these decades. Yet in this hidden season, the Word made flesh was growing "in wisdom and stature, and in favor with God and man" (Luke 2:52). The silence was not empty—it was pregnant with purpose.

The silence of God is often misunderstood as abandonment, when it's actually an invitation to deeper intimacy. God withdraws the loud, obvious manifestations of His presence to draw us into more attentive listening. Like the prophet Elijah who found God not in the earthquake or fire but in the "still small voice" (1 Kings 19:12), you learn to discern the whisper of the Spirit in the silence.

The Psalms are filled with honest cries from those who felt God's silence: "Do not be silent to me, lest I become like those who go down to the pit" (Psalm 28:1). Yet these same psalms usually end with renewed trust: "The Lord has heard my supplication; the Lord will receive my prayer" (Psalm 6:9). This pattern teaches us that divine silence tests and ultimately strengthens our faith.

There is a holy hush before the unveiling of every God-story. Think of Hannah, who prayed in wordless desperation in the temple, her lips moving but voice unheard by others. Heaven heard her. In her silence, a prophet was conceived. Think of Mary, who carried the Word of God in her womb in the secrecy of a village, treasuring the promise in her heart before the world saw its fulfillment. Or Jesus Himself, hidden in Nazareth as a carpenter, Heaven's King in common clothes. The greatest miracles germinate in obscurity. What grows in the dark will one day bloom in the light.

I'll go deeper into this in a later chapter—especially how women of color, and Black women in particular, can learn to leverage the gift of hiddenness and invisibility. It's not about shrinking; it's about learning to build in plain sight.

So when the silence feels suffocating, remember: God is still growing something sacred beneath the surface. These next few exercises will help you anchor yourself when His voice seems faint and His hand feels hidden. Refer back to this as often as you need during your silent season and find strength in what Pappa's doing in your defining hour.

SACRED EXERCISE

• Fast from unnecessary noise: Reduce your intake of social media, entertainment, or conversations that distract from stillness.

• Journal your questions, not just your revelations: Let your confusion become a conversation with God.

• Revisit past words: Re-read old journal entries or prophecies and ask the Holy Spirit if anything remains unfulfilled or needs obedience.

• Create rhythms of worship: Establish a morning or evening altar—just five minutes of intentional praise and surrender can shift your atmosphere.

• Guard your confession: Speak life over your season, even when you don't understand it yet.

This season may be silent, but it is not stagnant. What feels like delay is often deep development. Let the quiet refine you—not disqualify you.

SACRED PRAYER | *Father, even in the silence, I know You are near. When I cannot trace Your hand, I choose to trust Your heart. Let the seed You've planted within me break open beneath the soil—unseen, yet alive. Teach me to treasure the hidden years as Mary did, and to grow quietly strong like Jesus in Nazareth. Form me in secret until it is time to reveal what You've prepared. Even now, let Heaven's harmony steady my soul. I rest in Your silence, knowing it is not Your absence. Amen.*

CHAPTER 8

CULTURAL BRANDING VS. CALLING

Not everything with reach has roots.

Today's culture beckons with neon signs and instant platforms: "Build your brand!" "Don't stay hidden!" It shouts that your worth is measured by visibility, by how soon you can announce, launch, and be applauded. But the Spirit inside you speaks differently: calling over culture, obedience over spectacle. There is a crossroads where you must choose to either chase the spotlight of branding or carry the torch of calling through the midnight hours. Remember, in the beginning was the Word, not the website. God's calling was never meant to be a performance for others; it is a covenant between you and Him.

See Jesus on the pinnacle of the temple, tempted by the enemy to throw Himself down just to prove He was the Son of God. He refused to trade the intimacy of His calling for a publicity stunt. He chose the path of obedience, even though it led through obscurity and ultimately to a cross, instead of exploiting His power for popularity.

In the hidden place, an altar is built—not of stones, but of surrendered dreams. You lay down the shiny plans you made, the logo designs, the launch strategies, and you pick up a hammer to build in secret what God gave you. Every act of obedience in obscurity is like oil pressed from the olive, rich and fragrant, saved for an appointed hour. So let this be your declaration in the dark:

DIVINE DECLARATION | *I decree that I embrace seasons of holy hiddenness as ordained paths of preparation, not as punishment or oversight. I declare that what God is building through me has roots that reach to bedrock, foundations that cannot be shaken by criticism or acclaim. The work of my hands carries eternal weight because it was formed in the womb of waiting, not in the frenzy of fast-tracking. In Jesus' name, I refuse shortcuts to visibility that would compromise the integrity of my calling.*

We live in an age where visibility is mistaken for validity, where follower counts are confused with Kingdom impact. The marketplace of attention has created a new temptation: to be known rather than to be formed. Yet Jesus repeatedly withdrew from crowds that wanted to crown Him prematurely (John 6:15). He understood what many modern believers struggle to grasp—platform without preparation produces pressure that deforms calling into performance.

Contemporary ministry culture can unwittingly adopt worldly metrics of success: size, speed, and spectacle. But when we study Scripture's pattern of leadership development, we find God frequently uses the wilderness (literal or metaphorical) to form His vessels. Moses needed forty years, David needed his caves, Elijah needed Cherith Brook, Paul needed Arabia.

There is a reason why I'm placing such strong emphasis on your identity, your integrity, and your calling.

The Father is not building your platform. He is building your character. The platform is merely the byproduct of a life yielded to His purposes. When Mary received the angelic announcement of bearing the Messiah, she didn't rush to create content or build awareness. Scripture tells us "she treasured up all these things and pondered them in her heart" (Luke 2:19). Carrying glory requires this same contemplative posture before public declaration.

SACRED EXERCISE

Every builder must discern the season they are in. Not every season is for birthing; some are for burying, resting, or retooling. Sacred discernment allows you to come into agreement with Heaven's timing instead of culture's pressure.

Ask yourself: Am I in a preparation season or a planting one? Is this a time to build or a time to be rebuilt?

Take a moment to reflect on the fruit, patterns, and pressures you've experienced lately. Are doors opening or closing? Is clarity increasing or decreasing? What spiritual rhythms are most present—prayer, rest, repentance, revelation?

Rather than reacting to the noise around you, center yourself in God's current invitation. He never moves without purpose—and neither should you.

Prayerfully determine your current season and align your expectations and actions accordingly. Remember that even mature ministries cycle through these seasons repeatedly at different levels.

CHAPTER 9

BUILDERS ARE BIRTHING

You're not overwhelmed—you're crowning.

So you continue, a faithful builder working by lamplight, blueprint in one hand and sword in the other. There are nights the weight of this unseen work feels like travail. Indeed, builders are birthing. The blueprint God gave you is not just a project; it is a living thing hewn in the Spirit, and bringing it forth is a labor of love. You carry within you a vision, a promise, a piece of God's Kingdom waiting to be born.

Feel the Holy Spirit's encouragement like a midwife at your side. Do not fear the contractions; they are signs of life. The tightening you feel, the discomfort and stretching, are evidence that something new is on the verge. All of creation understands this pain-tinged hope. As the apostle wrote, "We know that the whole creation has been groaning as in the pains of childbirth until now," waiting for the revealing of God's children (Romans 8:22).

There is a divine timing to birth. In the fullness of time, what God planted in darkness begins to crown. Just as a baby's head crowns in the birth canal, the outline of your destiny presses against the threshold of this world. When a baby is about to be born, the labor intensifies, with waves coming closer together. If you have felt the intensity increase, take heart: These are not death pangs, but birth pangs. The opposition, the delays, the wrestling prayer—these are your spiritual contractions signaling imminent joy.

"Shall I bring to the point of birth and not deliver?" says the Lord. "Shall I who cause to bring forth shut the womb?" (Isaiah 66:9). No, He will not fail to bring forth what He planted. The God who authors life will also finish what He started in you.

Throughout Scripture, birthing metaphors appear when describing spiritual breakthrough. This reveals a profound truth: Kingdom manifestation follows the pattern of natural birth: conception, gestation, labor, and delivery. In Church history, every great revival followed this pattern. Before the Welsh Revival of 1904-1905, Evan Roberts spent years in prayer. Before Azusa Street poured out Pentecostal fire, William Seymour spent weeks in intense prayer and fasting. The labor preceded the delivery.

Your assignment carries this same divine DNA. What feels like overwhelming pressure is actually Kingdom convergence—Heaven pressing against Earth through your surrendered life. The weight is not crushing you, it's crowning through you.

SACRED EXERCISE

Find a quiet place. Set a Spirit-filled atmosphere that helps you sense Pappa's nearness. Place your hands over your abdomen as a prophetic act representing God's vision within you.

Ask the Holy Spirit to show you: What am I called to birth in this season? What has been incubating in the quiet, waiting for a release?

Let your prayer be one of agreement: "Lord, I yield to Your timing. I trust the contractions of transition. I declare that what You placed inside me will not be delayed, sabotaged, or aborted. I come into agreement with Your divine delivery schedule."

Even now, release the sound of faith. Speak what you're expecting. Declare the fruit of your obedience. This is not the time to question—this is the time to push.

CHAPTER 10

ARISE & SHINE

This is your altar moment.
Heaven is calling your name.

The time has come to rise from the shadows. The Holy Spirit is gently but firmly lifting you to your feet. It's your moment of emergence. Even now, the Lord Himself places a mantle over your shoulders—a garment woven with the threads of your trials and triumphs. It is the mantle of identity and authority, marked by your hidden journey with Him. The hiddenness was preparing you to wear this mantle with humility and power. The silence was teaching you to hear His whisper above the crowd's roar.

Rise now from the ashes of obscurity, daughter of Zion. This is not presumption, it is obedience. To remain hidden now would be to bury what God has unearthed. The season of preparation has yielded to the season of proclamation. Like Esther who prepared in secret before entering the king's court, you have been anointed "for such a time as this" (Esther 4:14).

Remember Moses at the burning bush? He argued his inadequacy until God finally asked, "Who gave human beings their mouths?" (Exodus 4:11). The One who called you has also equipped you. Your imperfections do not disqualify you, they authenticate your testimony. Like the Japanese art of Kintsugi, where broken pottery is repaired with gold, your healed fractures now gleam with divine light. Your scars have become stars that guide others through their own dark nights.

Hear this clearly: Your rising is not about personal elevation but Kingdom demonstration. You are not ascending a platform but a cross. True visibility requires greater vulnerability. When Jesus rode into Jerusalem on what we call Palm Sunday, the crowds cheered, but He knew the coronation they offered was incomplete. True enthronement would come through crucifixion. So it is with you—visibility without sacrifice lacks substance.

Let this be more than reflection—respond now to what Heaven is placing upon you.

SACRED EXERCISE

Stand with arms outstretched, ready to receive the mantle the Father is placing upon your shoulders.

Take a selah moment and posture yourself in prayer:

"Lord, I stand ready to receive what You have prepared for this season."

Now, in the stillness, allow yourself to see it. Imagine the Lord gently placing His mantle upon your shoulders. What does it feel like? Is it soft, weighty, royal? What colors or textures surround you? Let your spirit respond before your mind tries to explain.

Then ask, with open expectation:

"Holy Spirit, what does this mantle represent? What authority or anointing does it carry?"

You may not hear it all at once. You may feel a word, an impression, or a sudden clarity. Whatever comes—hold it as holy.

Now make this prophetic declaration with bold humility:

"I receive this mantle not by my merit but by Your mercy. I will wear it with humility and steward it with integrity."

And as you do, let the hesitation fall away. Let the fear of being seen, the doubt of being ready, and the lie of being too much or not enough—all bow at the feet of truth. This mantle is not about perfection. It's about permission. Heaven's permission. And you're not just covered—you're commissioned.

CHAPTER 11

THE COMMISSION AWAITS

The mantle you wear is not just for decoration
—it's for demonstration.

With the mantle comes the commission. Just as Jesus told His disciples, "As the Father has sent me, I am sending you" (John 20:21), He now commissions you. This is not a promotion but a progression—the natural next step in your spiritual journey.

What is a commission? It is both authorization and assignment. The centurion understood this when he told Jesus, "I myself am a man under authority, with soldiers under me. I tell this one, 'Go,' and he goes" (Matthew 8:9). Authority flows to those who know how to come under it. Your commission carries Heaven's authority because you have learned to bow before Heaven's throne.

A commission always contains these elements:

1. Clear identity – knowing who you are determines what you do

2. Defined territory – understanding your specific sphere of influence

3. Delegated authority – operating with Heaven's backing in your assignment

4. Kingdom purpose – advancing God's agenda, not personal ambition

Your assignment is not just a task but a territory—a sphere where Heaven's reality is meant to manifest through your obedience. As you step into this commission, carry both humility and boldness. Jesus displayed both when He washed His disciples' feet and when He cleansed the temple. This apparent paradox—servant leadership with unflinching authority—is the mark of true Kingdom ambassadors.

SACRED EXERCISE

Take a moment and imagine what might be written on your scroll. What names, nations, or industries are tied to your yes? What language is inscribed in Heaven's ink about your assignment?

You don't need to make something happen. Just agree with what has already been spoken. The scroll is in motion—your alignment activates it.

Now, as we turn the page to Section 2, we will explore this critical truth: Sacred Identity is Heaven's Prerequisite for lasting impact. The commissioning you've received must be built upon the unshakable foundation of knowing whose you are before understanding what you're to do.

Your journey continues—from crowning to commissioning to the sacred identity that sustains it all ...

Sacred Identity

HEAVEN'S PREREQUISITE

CHAPTER 12

ARISE IN YOUR DIVINE IDENTITY

"But you are a chosen people, a royal priesthood, a holy nation, God's special possession..." (1 Peter 2:9). From the outset, Heaven names you: royal and priestly. You are both a daughter of the King and a servant in His temple. This dual identity—king and priest—is the foundation for your calling.

Let's unpack that. As a priest, you carry intimacy with God; as royalty, you carry authority from God. Intimacy and authority—both are essential to your destiny. If you only embrace priesthood, you might say "I'll just stay hidden with God" and never step out to lead. If you only see yourself as royalty, you might grasp for authority without the grounding of relationship. God designed you to be both. You minister to Him in the secret place (priest) and you minister for Him in the public space (king). That's sacred identity: knowing you belong in both the throne room *and* the marketplace, in worship *and* in leadership.

Consider Esther. She wore a crown (royalty) but also called her people to fast and pray (priesthood). Her influence flowed from her intimacy. Or consider Deborah. She heard from God under the palm tree (priestly prophetic role) and then led the nation to victory (royal leadership role). Scripture overflows with this pattern of dual identity.

The enemy fiercely attacks this "priest-king" identity. He'll either try to make you doubt your authority ("Who am I to lead?") or undermine your intimacy ("I'm too busy to pray"). But when you know who you are—God's beloved daughter who carries both His name and His authority—you become unstoppable. You walk into meetings carrying the atmosphere of Heaven, and you pray with the confidence of one whom the King backs up. You can intercede like Hannah *and* strategize like Deborah. That's the power of knowing you are both royal and priestly.

Throughout history, whenever God prepared someone for a great assignment, He affirmed their identity. When God called Jeremiah as a prophet to the nations, He began not with tasks but with identity: "Before I formed you in the womb I knew you, before you were born I set you apart" (Jeremiah 1:5). God affirmed who Jeremiah was before He instructed him on what to do. Identity precedes assignment, always. In the same way, Heaven wants you secure in who you are before you step fully into what you must do.

So pause here. Hear the Father speaking over you: "You are My beloved daughter, in whom I delight." Let that sink in. That is the unshakeable foundation of your identity. You are not an orphan scrambling for approval; you are a beloved child of God. Everything else you build will rest on this foundation.

CHAPTER 13

THE MELCHIZEDEK ANOINTING

This dual royal-priestly identity finds its biblical archetype in Melchizedek, who was "king of Salem" and "priest of God Most High" (Genesis 14:18). This mysterious figure, reappearing in Hebrews as a type of Christ, embodied the union of authority and intimacy in one person. Christ Himself now holds this dual office perpetually (Hebrews 7:17), and remarkably, He shares this same dual nature with His church.

When you begin to walk in your Melchizedek anointing—both royal and priestly—you no longer feel forced to choose between soaking in His presence and showing up in your calling. The spiritual rhythm of receiving in His presence and releasing in your spheres of authority becomes the heartbeat of authentic ministry.

Church history shows the danger of separating these two aspects. When royalty functions without priesthood, leadership becomes tyrannical and self-serving. When priesthood functions without royalty, spiritual communities become insular and ineffective. This integrated identity was not only reflected in the life of William Wilberforce, whose deep devotional life fueled his parliamentary fight against the transatlantic slave trade. Across history, countless Black abolitionists, pastors, and prophets stood on both prayer grounds and battlefields to dismantle systems of oppression, showing us that sacred intimacy and strategic justice work hand-in-hand.

Think of Sojourner Truth, whose fiery preaching and relentless advocacy for abolition and women's rights flowed directly from her encounters with the living God. Or Bishop Desmond Tutu, who carried his pastoral heart into the public square to help dismantle apartheid through both intercession and activism. In fact, think of Jehoshaphat, who established both worship and governance reforms throughout Judah. Or Lydia in the New Testament, whose commercial leadership (selling purple cloth) complemented her spiritual hospitality (hosting the church). These examples consistently demonstrate the symbiotic relationship between priestly intimacy and royal administration.

SACRED PRAYER | *Father God, I come before You in the name of Jesus, acknowledging that You alone have the right to name me. You conceived me before time began. You formed me with purpose. You redeemed me at great cost.*

I renounce every false identity I have embraced. I reject the names given to me by trauma, criticism, rejection, failure, comparison, and shame. These are not my true names. I cancel their authority over my thoughts, emotions, decisions, and destiny.

Jesus, You who hung on a cross with a mocking sign above Your head yet knew exactly who You were, give me that same unshakable grasp of my true identity. Let Your voice drown out all competing voices.

Holy Spirit, reveal to me the specific name the Father calls me—that unique aspect of His character I was created to reflect. Help me recognize when I'm operating from false identity rather than true identity.

I receive my position as Your beloved child, Your royal priesthood, Your holy vessel. When the enemy whispers, "Who do you think you are?" I will answer confidently, "I am who Heaven says I am."

Establish me so firmly in this truth that my very presence calls others into their true identity. Let me be a carrier of Heaven's perspective, seeing others as You see them.

In Jesus' name, Amen.

CHAPTER 14

WHO TOLD YOU THAT?

When God asked Adam and Eve, "Who told you that you were na-ked?" (Genesis 3:11), He exposed the lies they had believed about themselves. Likewise, part of reclaiming your sacred identity is let-ting God confront the false names and labels you've internalized.

Perhaps at some point you picked up the name "Failure" because a business idea or ministry didn't succeed, or "Unworthy" because someone important rejected you. Maybe "Not Enough" became a script in your mind due to comparisons with others.

Speaking of scripts—during my time on the "tell-a-vision" news team, I now realize how I directly and indirectly helped reinforce some of the very false narratives Heaven never approved. Day after day, we shaped headlines, filtered stories, and spotlighted only the most curated slices of life. And while media can inform and inspire, it also subtly scripts who we think we're supposed to be—fanning the flames of comparison, distortion, and quiet shame.

But after my own personal Damascus Road journey, I learned to reject the narratives that don't come from Heaven, and now I help others do the same.

This journey is about exchanging lies for truth.

And this is not about positive thinking, it's spiritual warfare over your identity. Those false labels are like sticky notes on your soul that need the Holy Spirit's solvent to remove. It might be a process—sometimes the glue is strong! But persist. Each time an old label whispers, answer it out loud with God's Word: "Actually, I am a new creation in Christ. I am chosen and appointed by God. I am more than a conqueror through Him who loves me." The Word of God washes away what is not of Him.

Take Gideon as an example. He saw himself as the least in his family, insignificant and afraid, hiding in a winepress. But when an angel of the Lord appeared, the greeting was, "The Lord is with you, mighty warrior" (Judges 6:12). Gideon probably looked around, confused. *Who, me?* God spoke identity into him that didn't match his feelings. Gideon had to decide which voice to believe. Eventually, he agreed with God and indeed became a mighty warrior who delivered Israel.

So ask yourself who told you the names you've been answering to. If it wasn't God, then you don't have to own them. Heaven has the final say on your identity. Let God rename you where needed. Abram became Abraham (father of nations), Jacob became Israel (prince with God), Simon became Peter (rock). God's truth about you uproots the enemy's lies about you. He calls Gideon, who's hiding in a winepress, a "mighty warrior" (Judges 6:12). He calls timid

Jeremiah a prophet to nations and knew him before birth (Jeremiah 1:5). When God speaks, His Word creates reality. Gideon indeed becomes a mighty warrior; Jeremiah does boldly prophesy.

The pattern is clear: Heaven names, then Heaven empowers. We must cooperate by rejecting any identity not from God. This might mean confronting painful words spoken over you in the past by parents, teachers, or even church leaders that didn't align with what God says. It might mean forgiving those who misnamed you, and embracing the name "daughter."

This isn't something I walk around talking about often, but I pray that sharing my personal testimony strengthens you and offers a trusted reassurance: I'm all in with you.

I get it.
I see you.
I understand.

My heart is full knowing we get to share space together—lifting each other up in prayer, carrying one another in love, and standing on the promise that while our Father never said this walk would be easy, He did promise never to leave us.

For me, one of the deepest wounds I carried was not knowing who my natural father was. Growing up, I remember whispers: that he struggled with the idea of being a father, or that he was said to have made other suggestions at the time.

Mom, if you're reading this, please know—I understand this may be hard to see written out. But God ... God kept us both. And if I've never said it before, let me say it now: thank you.

Thank you for refusing to heed any voices that may have tried to nudge you toward what seemed the easier way. And thank you to my dad, who helped raise me as his own.

Years later, after I moved to the Carolinas, my husband and I were sorting through old storage boxes. I stumbled across my birth certificate—a document I'd seen before, but never really studied. This time, though, my eyes locked on one specific space: the box where my father's name should have been.

Blank.

That empty space stared back at me, and for a moment, I felt all the cold, sterile emotions of being unwanted, unworthy, and not enough.

How could someone not want to claim this amazing little bundle of joy—ME? (Smile.)

But right there, in that quiet moment of staring at the blank space, Pappa God ministered to me so deeply and so tenderly.

I sensed Him whispering in my spirit: "I signed My name. Before you were even formed, I wanted you. You are not a mistake. You are Mine. And you are loved, by your Father."

That was the moment everything shifted.

That was the day I forever became a Daddy's Girl.

Author's Note: Since writing this, God, the Author and Finisher of our faith, has written a chapter I never saw coming: a miraculous reconnection with my biological father's family. Meeting his sister after many years brought tears, joy, and stories that offered a tender kind of closure. Some details of the past differ, but being remembered and embraced only confirmed what the Father had long spoken to me: that I was known, wanted, and loved.

CHAPTER 15

THE ARCHAEOLOGY OF FALSE IDENTITY

False identities don't show up out of nowhere. They get layered into our lives one experience, one word, one disappointment at a time.

Think of it like spiritual archaeology. These false names get buried deep, sometimes under years of memories, pain, or pressure. And unearthing them isn't about rushing or ripping things up—it's about letting the Holy Spirit, your personal Master Archaeologist, gently walk you back through what was buried, so He can begin to rebuild what was broken.

As the Spirit begins to uncover buried layers, you may find that false identities often form in a few familiar places. You may see yourself in one—or several—of the following:

- **Trauma narratives:** Pain has a way of shaping identity, especially when survival becomes the focus. If you were abandoned, you may have adopted "Unwanted" as a kind of shield against future rejection. If you were abused, "Damaged" might have felt like the only way to make sense of your pain. Trauma doesn't just leave bruises. It can re-name you. But the good news? Jesus knows how to rewrite every name pain ever gave you.

- **Authority declarations:** When people in positions of pow-er speak, we tend to listen—even when what they say is far from true. Maybe a parent told you, "You're too much." A teacher once said, "You'll never be anything." A spiritual leader implied you were too broken to be used. Whether they meant it or not, those words had weight. And if we're not careful, they echo louder than Heaven's voice.

- **Cultural messaging:** This one is sneaky, because it's ev-erywhere. Culture says, "You're only valuable if you look like this, earn like that, live here, or have that." Social media says, "Be the best version of yourself, but only if it fits the aesthetic." So we start wearing names like "Not Enough" or "Almost There But Never Quite."

- **Religious distortions:** Let's be honest—sometimes the deepest wounds come from warped theology. If you were taught that God is always disappointed in you, or your rela-tionship with Him was filtered through fear, performance, or shame, you might have picked up false names like "Perpetual Letdown," "Divine Disappointment," "Heaven's Disgrace," or "Invisible." Hear this clearly: That is not the heart of the Father. And the God of grace is ready to re-store your name.

Why does the origin of these identities matter? Because where the identity came from often determines how it needs to be healed. A trauma-rooted identity will require different care than one formed by culture or comparison. Thankfully, the Holy Spirit knows exactly where the break happened, and He's dedicated to walking with you through every layer until the true you is uncovered.

CHAPTER 16

IDENTITY WARFARE: DEFENDING YOUR NAME

Make no mistake—this is a war for your name. But the weapons of our warfare are not carnal. They are mighty through God, and they begin with agreement: agreement with what He has spoken, and resistance to anything else.

If identity is your inheritance, then these practices are the way you defend it—not through striving, but through sustained agreement with Heaven. Here are rhythms I return to when identity warfare rises up:

- **Scripture immersion:** Truth has to live in your spirit and in your mouth. Don't just read the Word, meditate on verses that speak directly to your identity in Christ. Highlight them. Write them down. Stick them on your mirror. Let Heaven's language become your internal script.

- **Declaration practice:** Your mouth is a weapon. Speak your true identity out loud. Daily. Even when it feels awkward or unnatural. Your spirit responds to sound. So do the lies.

Faith comes through hearing—and that includes hearing yourself declare who you really are.

- **Community confirmation:** You need people who can see you and speak to the real you, especially when you forget. Surround yourself with people who remind you who you are in God, not just what you do. Their encouragement will become a lifeline when old lies try to creep back in.

- **Testimonial documentation:** When you start seeing fruit from living in your true identity, write it down. Journal the wins, the breakthroughs, the moments you showed up as your God-authored self. These testimonies will anchor you when doubt or warfare tries to pull you under.

- **Trigger response protocols:** Let's be practical. When the lies resurface—and they will—don't be caught off guard. Create a go-to strategy: a prayer, a verse, a friend you text, a worship playlist, a quiet space. Know in advance how to fight when the old script starts to play.

You were never meant to fight for your identity alone. You've got Heaven's backing, a new name, and a strategy. On this journey, you're not just reclaiming your voice—you're learning to protect it.

The Apostle Paul modeled this kind of identity warfare. When he wrote, "I no longer live, but Christ lives in me" (Galatians 2:20), that wasn't some passive resignation. That was a revelation Paul understood what it meant to lay down the false names, the religious pride, the shame of his past, the labels people tried to stick on him, and fully embrace who he was in Christ.

His letters are full of that language:

In Christ
New creation
Children of God
Saints
Beloved

He wasn't just preaching identity, he was reinforcing it. Over and over again. Like a warrior guarding something set apart. Because he knew when you really know who you are, you become dangerous to the darkness.

And so do you.

SACRED EXERCISE

Take a moment to reflect on your life like a timeline—a journey full of moments, both hard and holy, that have shaped how you see yourself.

Some of those moments may have left painful imprints. Others may have affirmed something true and beautiful about who you are. In this gentle exercise, we're inviting the Holy Spirit to walk with you while you revisit some of those identity markers—not to relive the pain, but to reclaim the truth.

Are there moments that shaped how you see yourself

—for better or worse. Jot down one false name that still tries to linger and one truth from God's Word that sets the record straight. What would it look like to agree with Heaven today?

Let this be a conversation between you and the Father—a divine exchange. You're not just revisiting your past; you're rewriting your perspective. You're partnering with the Holy Spirit to reclaim every label, every season, and every part of your becoming.

You are not who life said you were. You are who He says you are.

This transformation doesn't occur instantaneously but progressively as the Holy Spirit applies the finished work of adoption to your heart. Jesus addressed this very process in the parable of the Prodigal Son (Luke 15:11-32), which actually portrays two sons with orphan mentalities—one through rebellion, one through religion—and neither fully experiencing sonship despite their father's abundant love.

We've even seen this same kind of identity shift in Church history.

Take Martin Luther, for example. He was a Christian leader who lived in the 1500s, and for a long time, like many people of his day, he believed he had to earn God's love by being perfect, following strict religious rules, and doing everything "right."

But after a deep, personal encounter with Scripture, God opened his eyes to something life-changing: we are made right with God not by earning it, but by simply believing and receiving His grace.

That shift was huge. It moved the Church from a mindset of "I have to prove I'm good enough for God" to "I get to receive God's love because of Jesus."

Martin Luther even came up with a phrase that still helps people today. He said we are "simultaneously sinners and saints." What he meant was yes, we're still growing. Yes, we still mess up. But at the same time, we are fully loved, fully accepted, and fully seen by God.

It's like this: You don't have to wait until you've "arrived" to belong in God's family. He calls you His daughter right now, and as you walk with Him, the Holy Spirit gently helps you grow into all you've been called to be.

CHAPTER 17

THE NEW NAME

In Revelation 2:17, Jesus promises to give the overcomer "a white stone with a new name written on it, known only to the one who receives it." This hints that God has a specific identity for you that perhaps no one fully sees yet—even you. It's unique, precious, and will be revealed in greater fullness as you overcome lies and walk closely with Him.

Ask God in prayer, "Father, what name do You call me?" He may remind you of a Scripture or a quality, or speak a word into your heart. It could be "My Brave One" or "Faithful" or "Pure Heart" or any number of affirmations. However He speaks, cherish that. Write it down. Let that name define you more than any human label ever could.

One woman might hear "Esther" because she's called to courageous influence; another might hear "Mary" because she carries a heart of devotion and will birth things through surrender. God has a way of communicating our identity in ways that resonate deeply.

Let the Holy Spirit reframe how you see yourself. This is part of renewing your mind (Romans 12:2). It's not prideful to agree with God; it's actually humility. If He says you're forgiven, strong, chosen, humility says, "Amen, Lord, it is so," rather than arguing with Him.

A Consecrated Invitation: Receive the Name God Calls You *(You may want to save this for a quiet moment later—or let the Spirit lead you now.)*

5. **Preparation phase.** Set aside uninterrupted time (at least thirty minutes) in a quiet space. Begin with worship that focuses on God's character rather than your needs.

6. **Scripture meditation.** Read Revelation 2:17, Isaiah 62:2–5, and Isaiah 43:1–7, asking the Holy Spirit to illuminate these passages specifically for you.

7. **Listening prayer.** Ask: "Father, what name do You call me? What aspect of Your nature have You particularly designed me to reflect?" Then sit in receptive silence, not straining but attentive.

8. **Documented discernment.** Write down impressions, words, images, or Scriptures that come to mind without immediately analyzing or dismissing them.

9. **Confirmation seeking.** Share what you received with trusted spiritual mentors or friends who know you well, asking if it resonates with what they perceive in you.

10. **Living activation.** Begin prayerfully stepping into this name, asking God to develop its fullness in your character and calling.

Remember, this name might be revealed in stages rather than all at once. It might initially come as a characteristic ("Faithful," "Courageous") before developing into greater specificity.

HEAVEN'S BRIDGE | *As your sacred identity becomes firmly established in the foundation of Heaven's perspective, you naturally begin to inquire, "What has God entrusted to me to steward?" Just as a beloved daughter receives an inheritance from her father, you too have received a supernatural endowment from your Heavenly Father—unique gifts, talents, and capacities placed within you before birth. These are not random abilities but purposeful deposits aligned with your divine assignment. In the next section, we'll explore how to discover, develop, and deploy these gifts as we continue the journey from identity to purpose, uncovering the treasures Heaven has hidden within you.*

The Gifts Within

DISCOVERING YOUR SACRED ENDOWMENT

CHAPTER 18

THE ETERNAL INTEGRATION OF SPIRITUAL GIFTS

Heaven has not only healed your identity, it has commissioned your gifts. As you step forward, you must understand not only *who* you are, but *how* you've been divinely equipped for impact.

In fact, you're stepping into a section of this book that was birthed through one of the most intentional conversations I've ever had with God. I literally sat down and interviewed the Holy Ghost—pen in hand, questions pouring from my spirit. I was desperate to know the "what."

What did You place in me before time began?
What am I supposed to do with it now?

That moment marked a turning point. Suddenly, Daddy began shining a light on things I had overlooked—old journal entries, repeated life patterns, insights from mentors, even my training as a journalist. All of it was connected. What I thought was just curiosity became divine intel. What I thought was research became revelation.

I didn't realize it at the time, but the Holy Spirit was walking me through a blueprint, not only for me, but for others too.

What emerged wasn't just insight about spiritual gifts, it was the early framework for what you're holding now. A tool. A language. A Holy Spirit–breathed map of our supernatural DNA. And I was simply an available and curious vessel He chose to birth it through.

The next stage of our journey unveils your Sacred Identity™ Signature Gift Set—the convergence of motivation, ministry, and supernatural manifestation Heaven embedded within you. Scripture reveals this three-fold design throughout its pages.

When David faces Goliath, we see the convergence of his leadership motivation (ruler), his pastoral ministry function (shepherd), and the manifestation gifts of supernatural faith and divine power that brought victory.

When Esther stood for her people, her mercy-driven motivation stirred intercession. She rose into an apostolic ministry function, executing kingdom authority through governmental influence. And her breakthrough came through the manifestation of divine wisdom released at just the right time.

"For we are His workmanship, created in Christ Jesus for good works, which God prepared beforehand, that we should walk in them" (Ephesians 2:10).

The word "workmanship" comes from the Greek word "poiēma," meaning "masterpiece" or "poem." You are God's artistry in motion, designed not just for church activity, but for divine influence in every sphere of life.

Think of your gifting architecture as a three-dimensional design.

MOTIVATIONAL GIFTS ACTIVATION

Ask the Holy Spirit: What gift anchors my motivation and approach to people and problems? Am I wired to encourage, teach, serve, lead, give, show mercy, or perceive spiritually?

Pay attention to what energizes you versus what drains you. The grace God placed within you should bear fruit and feel aligned.

MINISTRY GIFTS ACTIVATION

Invite the Lord to highlight where He is placing you within the Body. Do you sense a pull toward teaching, pastoring, evangelizing, apostolic leadership, or prophetic encouragement?

You may see glimpses through your influence, voice, or burden for others. Let this activation be a mirror, not a label.

Remember, ministry gifts don't only show up behind a pulpit, they also lead, build, and shepherd in boardrooms, classrooms, kitchens, and communities.

MANIFESTATION GIFTS ACTIVATION

Ask the Holy Spirit to reveal which manifestation gifts flow when you're surrendered in prayer, worship, or ministry. Have you witnessed healing, tongues, prophecy, discernment, or supernatural wisdom flowing through you?

These are not earned, they are distributed as the Spirit wills. Your only posture is availability and discernment.

When these three layers align, you don't just function, you *flow*. Your motivational gift fuels your passion. Your ministry function gives it direction. And your manifestation gifts release Heaven's power for real impact.

This is why some women serve tirelessly yet still feel unfulfilled—they're missing part of the equation. They know their passion, but not their power. They know their calling, but haven't discerned their supernatural tools. And they wonder why it all feels off.

This was never the Father's design.

At a recent workshop, one woman in her seventies pulled me aside with tears in her eyes. "I thought life had passed me by," she said. "But now I see—I just didn't know who I really was." Another participant whispered, "Please let me know when Sacred Identity™ is ready. I so need this in my life."

These women didn't attend a product launch—they encountered the power of prophetic clarity. When Heaven reveals your spiritual blueprint, age, background, or status don't disqualify you. They become proof that your divine timing has come. Your Sacred Identity™ Signature Gift Set was calibrated by Heaven for impact that goes far beyond Sunday service. You are an ambassador, a Kingdom representative, equipped to bring divine solutions into boardrooms, classrooms, city councils, creative spaces, family systems, and everywhere the world is groaning for transformation.

This is what Paul was speaking to when he described us as the "ekklesia," the called-out ones. In the original Greek, that word didn't describe a church building; it referred to a governing body, a people sent out to legislate, represent, and enact the will of the King. You are part of Heaven's transition team, God's chosen ambassadors assigned to bring Kingdom realities into broken systems and waiting cities. You weren't saved just to sit. You were sent to shift.

God never meant for your gifts to stay locked exclusively in the pews. He designed them to rebuild, restore, and reform the places He's sending you.

CHAPTER 19

MOTIVATIONAL GIFTS—YOUR SPIRITUAL WIRING

These seven motivational gifts from Romans 12 reveal how you naturally perceive needs and respond to people. They form the foundation of your spiritual wiring and how you instinctively view the world.

1. **Prophet (aka Perceiver):** You instinctively discern truth from falsehood and naturally speak truth that brings alignment. This is about how you perceive reality—not a public office or spiritual utterance. (We'll explore the Five-Fold ministry gifts and manifestation gifts in the coming pages.)

2. **Server:** You notice practical needs others overlook and find deep fulfillment in meeting those needs with excellence and without recognition.

3. **Teacher:** You naturally research, organize information, and present truth systematically so others can understand complex concepts.

4. **Exhorter:** You innately see potential in others and naturally encourage and urge others forward into their purpose with hope and practical steps.

5. **Giver:** You instinctively recognize resource needs and steward provision with supernatural wisdom, understanding the spiritual dynamics of generosity.

6. **Leader (aka Organizer/Administrator):** You naturally organize people and processes, seeing the steps needed to implement vision with excellence and sustainability.

7. **Mercy:** You genuinely feel the emotions of others and create atmospheres of healing comfort where the wounded find true restoration.

Consider how Mary of Bethany demonstrated the mercy motivation when she sat at Jesus' feet, while Martha revealed her leader-administrator motivation. Both were expressing their God-given wiring, though one needed realignment in that moment. These motivational gifts shape your emotional and relational instincts from childhood; they are the bedrock of how you respond to the world around you.

In the marketplace, your motivational gift doesn't change, it simply expresses itself in different environments. A prophet (perceiver) becomes the truth-teller, the one who names what others ignore and brings alignment where there's drift. In corporate or ministry settings, they expose blind spots and uphold integrity where outcomes depend on reality, not illusion. A server becomes the operations powerhouse, ensuring excellence behind the scenes with precision others overlook. Every motivation becomes a Kingdom lens for solving problems, leading teams, and stewarding influence.

SACRED EXERCISE

Which of these seven motivations resonates most deeply with how you naturally respond to life, people, and problems? Ask a few trusted friends or mentors what gift they consistently see operating in you. Sometimes the people around us can spot our strength more clearly than we can.

You might find yourself thinking, "Honestly, all of these feel familiar." And it's true—you may carry strong secondary or even third-layer motivations. But when it comes to your foundational gift, there is typically one that stands out. It's the one that shapes how you see, serve, and show up in the world.

If you're still unsure, that's okay. You're not alone. I walked through the same journey: praying, asking, journaling, and second-guessing before I finally downloaded and transcribed the blueprint Daddy was placing in my spirit.

If you're ready for more clarity, the Sacred Identity™ tool is available to help you fast-track the process. It's a guided resource designed to help you discern the lead gift Heaven wired into your design from the very beginning.

Because once you're clear on that, everything—how you live, love, lead, and build—begins to make sense.

 *To learn more or begin the experience, scan the QR code or visit **TheSacredBusiness.com** to access your Sacred Identity™ Signature Gift Set.*

MINISTRY GIFTS / FIVE-FOLD OFFICES—YOUR PUBLIC FUNCTION

"And He Himself gave some to be apostles, some prophets, some evangelists, and some pastors and teachers, for the equipping of the saints for the work of ministry, for the edifying of the body of Christ" (Ephesians 4:11–12).

Traditionally, the five-fold ministry gifts have been taught within the context of church leadership. And yes, they do equip the Body in formal ministry settings. But that's not where their influence ends. In fact, that's not even where their original meaning began.

As we discussed earlier, the word "church" that Jesus used wasn't religious at all—it was "ekklesia," a governmental term. It described a body of people called out to legislate, influence, and implement the culture of a Kingdom within a territory. While the sanctuary cultivates and equips us, the five-fold gifts were never meant to remain confined to it. These gifts were designed to move fluidly through homes, businesses, schools, and culture. You are part of that ekklesia. You are part of God's Kingdom transition team sent to shift atmospheres, restore foundations, and bring the culture of Heaven wherever you're assigned.

Whether you're building systems, starting nonprofits, leading teams, raising children, or launching vision in the marketplace, your five-fold function still applies. You are just as apostolic in the board-room as someone is in the pulpit. Just as pastoral over your team as a shepherd is over their flock. Just as prophetic in your business strategy as someone else may be in their intercession. The setting may shift. But the function remains the same.

Here's how these gifts can show up beyond traditional ministry roles:

Apostle — Governs. You may be called to pioneer new systems, launch platforms, build organizations, or establish structures others will grow from. Apostles function as master builders, and that includes founding schools, nonprofits, coaching platforms, tech innovations, or strategic networks.

Prophet — Guides. You may receive divine insight and foresight in business planning, community advocacy, or cultural discernment. Prophets are God's eyes and ears, whether in strategy rooms, media studios, or social justice movements. You release truth and alignment wherever you go.

Evangelist — Gathers. You may carry a contagious energy that draws people together. Evangelists thrive in outreach, community building, and promotional work. Whether you're leading events, building visibility, or activating others, your presence creates passion and points people toward the Truth.

Pastor — Guards. You're the protector, the nurturer, the safe place. Pastors in the marketplace show up as culture carriers, building emotionally safe environments, leading with compassion, and creating cohesion and care in teams, clients, or communities.

Teacher — Grounds. You're the clarifier. The explainer. The one who turns complex concepts into clear pathways. Teachers show up powerfully as content creators, coaches, curriculum designers, instructors, and mentors, grounding others in truth with wisdom and patience.

Don't count yourself out just because your ministry-level gift doesn't "look" like church. God never asked you to perform it, only to carry it. You are not less spiritual because your assignment isn't on a stage. You are not less called because your workplace has cubicles instead of pews. You are not less prophetic because your downloads come in dreams, spreadsheets, or team meetings.

El Roi—the God Who Sees—sees you.

He sees your obedience in both sacred and seemingly small places. He sees how you guard your team, gather your community, guide your clients, ground your students, and govern the systems He's trusted to your care.

This is your ministry.
This is your mantle.
And yes—this is your moment.

As your motivational gift matures, it often begins to take on ministry form. A mercy-motivated daughter may begin to shepherd hearts. A perceiver-born one may find herself moving prophetically.

I'll never forget a moment during one of my webinars. The moment I unpacked the exhorter gift, a woman typed, *"This is confirming so much for me right now!"* In that instant, she recognized that her core motivation was exhortation, but her mantle was expressed through teaching. That's what alignment looks like—when your inner gift and outer calling finally agree.

These transitions from internal wiring to external expression don't happen by accident. They unfold through intentional stewardship, prayerful discernment, and divine appointment. The gift within is first awakened, then aligned, and eventually assigned for Kingdom deployment. I'll never forget what Juanelle Teague shared with me after hearing one of my early teachings. Juanelle isn't just any peer—she's a nationally recognized speech coach and the ghost-writer for the legendary Zig Ziglar himself. With decades of experience helping speakers clarify their voice and message, she told me:

"What you do is a deep well—most people stop at talent, but you help women tap into their spiritual gift and brilliance. Your skillset is more like a SUPERCHARGED anointing."

That encouragement wasn't about me—it was about the result of alignment. When a woman discerns her divine design, power flows naturally. And when that divine wiring is activated, it reaches deeper than branding or performance—it hits the spirit.

We see this clearly in Deborah. She carried the motivational gift of prophet—deeply intuitive, justice-oriented, and Spirit-led. But she didn't stop there. She stepped into the ministry offices of prophet and judge, governing her people with wisdom, strategy, and courage. Her internal design and her public assignment were in perfect agreement. That's why her leadership carried so much weight.

These five-fold gifts are not confined to a pulpit—they're Kingdom leadership models designed for both the church and the marketplace. They equip us to influence culture with conviction.

So pause here, Divine Daughter of God. Take a breath and ask yourself:

Which of these ministry expressions am I naturally drawn to? Where do I feel most alive when helping others grow? What kind of leadership flows from me when I'm simply being myself—Spirit-led and surrendered?

If you're not sure yet, that's okay. Ask someone who's walked with you in faith. Let them mirror back the mantle they see in you. Because trust me, it's there. It's been there.

And now ... it's time to step into it.

CHAPTER 21

MANIFESTATION GIFTS—YOUR SUPERNATURAL EMPOWERMENT

"But the manifestation of the Spirit is given to each one for the profit of all" (1 Corinthians 12:7).

If motivational gifts are your spiritual DNA, and five-fold ministry gifts are your public mantle, the manifestation gifts of the Holy Spirit are the power tools He places in your hands for real-time impact. These gifts don't flow from personality or position—but from proximity to the Spirit. Let's take a closer look at each one, starting with the Word of Wisdom.

Word of wisdom: Supernatural insight into applying knowledge with heaven's perspective, revealing divine solutions where human wisdom fails. Solomon demonstrated this when resolving the dispute between two women claiming the same baby (1 Kings 3:16-28). His solution transcended conventional judicial approaches.

Word of knowledge: Receiving specific information not learned through natural means, exposing hidden things for breakthrough. Jesus demonstrated this gift when He told the Samaritan woman details about her five previous husbands (John 4:16-19). His revelation bypassed human reasoning and pierced the heart with healing truth.

Faith: Supernatural certainty that transcends circumstances, creating an atmosphere where impossibilities surrender. Abraham believed God's promise despite his age and Sarah's barrenness (Romans 4:19–21). His confidence wasn't in the outcome, it was in the One who made the promise.

Gifts of healing: Divine power to restore physical, emotional, and spiritual health beyond medical explanation. Paul exercised this gift on the island of Malta, healing Publius' father and subsequently many others (Acts 28:7-9). His hands delivered what medicine couldn't, and mercy flowed through every touch.

Working of miracles: Supernatural intervention that suspends natural laws and demonstrates God's supreme authority. Elisha stretched himself over a dead boy, and the child came back to life (2 Kings 4:32–35). His obedient, Spirit-led act interrupted death itself and displayed the miraculous power of God working through yielded vessels.

Prophecy: Speaking divinely inspired words that reveal God's heart, building up, encouraging, and comforting His people. Agabus prophesied about a coming famine, allowing the church to prepare relief measures (Acts 11:27-30). His words didn't entertain curiosity, they awakened action before crisis arrived.

Discerning of spirits: Supernatural perception of the spiritual forces operating in a situation, person, or atmosphere. Peter discerned the deceptive spirit operating in Ananias and Sapphira (Acts 5:1-10). His perception pierced the mask, revealing what was hidden beneath the surface.

Different kinds of tongues: Speaking languages not learned naturally, whether human languages or spiritual prayer languages. The disciples exercised this gift on the Day of Pentecost when they spoke in various known languages and people from many nations heard the Gospel in their native tongue (Acts 2:1 12). Their language didn't come from study, it came from surrender.

Interpretation of tongues: Supernatural ability to interpret messages given in unknown tongues for the edification of all. Paul refers this gift in his instruction to the Corinthian church, emphasizing that tongues spoken in a gathering should be interpreted so the church may be built up (1 Corinthians 14:27–28). His insight turned mystery into message, translating Heaven's voice for Earth's understanding.

Unlike motivational gifts, which you consistently carry, manifestation gifts are distributed "to each one as the Spirit wills" (1 Corinthians 12:11). As mentioned earlier, think of them like power tools the Spirit lends you at needed moments. You might notice you use some more often than others; that's okay and often part of your purpose.

Like motivational gifts, these gifts are not confined to religious settings; they are also divine tools for marketplace transformation. The word of wisdom might manifest in a corporate boardroom during strategic planning. The gift of healing might operate through a medical professional or counselor. The gift of discernment might function through a judge presiding over a complex case. Words of knowledge might empower an educator to understand a student's unspoken needs. Divine faith might strengthen an entrepreneur facing impossible odds.

These gifts are tools of power for ministry. And you can ask for them. "Earnestly desire spiritual gifts," Paul urges, especially prophecy (1 Corinthians 14:1). It's not wrong to say, "Lord, I'm available. Use me in healing, or give me words of knowledge if You will." He loves a willing vessel.

The key is intimacy and motive. We don't chase gifts for show; we seek to love people effectively. Paul sandwiches the gifts teaching between 1 Corinthians 13 (love) and 1 Corinthians 14 (order in church), reminding us love is the aim and humble stewardship is the posture.

CHAPTER 22

OVERCOMING BARRIERS TO MANIFESTATION GIFTS

Let's be honest, many believers want to move in manifestation gifts but quietly wrestle with what's holding them back. And that's okay. God is not afraid of your questions, your past, or your personality. But He does want to heal anything that's standing in the way of His Spirit flowing through you.

Here are a few common barriers that may be lingering in your heart or mindset:

- **"I'm not sure if these gifts are even for today."** Maybe you've heard teaching that suggests manifestation gifts ended with the early church. But Scripture reminds us that the same Spirit who raised Christ from the dead still lives in you. His gifts didn't expire.

- **"What if it gets weird—or worse, fake?"** If you've seen emotional hype or manipulation in the name of the Spirit, it's natural to be cautious. But remember, the Holy Spirit is a Spirit of order *and* power. He doesn't need theatrics to move.

- **"What if I get it wrong?"** Fear of failure can paralyze you before you even try. But God isn't looking for perfection, just willingness. You grow by stepping out, not sitting back.

- **"That's just not my personality."** Some of us are quiet, introverted, or more analytical. And that's beautiful. The Holy Spirit works through who you are, not who someone else is. You don't have to be loud to be Spirit-led.

- **"What will people think if I do this at work or in public?"** Many of us compartmentalize the supernatural to Sunday mornings. But God moves just as powerfully in staff meetings, client calls, coffee shops, or courtrooms. Wisdom and boldness go hand in hand.

- **"I've been disappointed before."** Maybe you stepped out once and felt embarrassed or let down. Maybe nothing happened. But don't let one moment define your capacity. The enemy loves to use disappointment to shut down destiny. But God redeems every attempt made in faith.

Take a moment for gentle heart preparation:

"Holy Spirit, I make myself available as Your vessel. I desire to be used in manifestation gifts, not for personal significance, but to demonstrate Your love and power to others. Remove any hindrances in my heart—fear, pride, unbelief, or past disappointments. Create in me clean hands and a pure heart for Your use."

As you continue this journey, begin identifying what may still be holding you back. Ask yourself:

- What exactly am I afraid might happen?
- What lie am I believing about God, myself, or this gift?
- What scripture directly counters that fear or lie?

You don't have to answer everything today. But be honest with God and stay open.

Because the very thing you're nervous about may be the very place He wants to flow through you the most.

CHAPTER 23

THE SACRED IDENTITY™ SIGNATURE GIFT SET INTEGRATION

Divine, hear me well: These three gift dimensions were never meant to operate in isolation. They form one integrated spiritual design, your Sacred Identity™.

MOTIVATION (HEART) + MINISTRY (HANDS) + MANIFESTATION (POWER) = DESTINY FULFILLMENT

Consider these integrated gift patterns:

- A believer with the motivational gift of prophecy, functioning in the five-fold ministry of teaching, empowered by manifestation gifts of word of knowledge and discernment.

- A believer with the motivational gift of mercy, functioning in the five-fold ministry of pastor, empowered by manifestation gifts of healing and word of wisdom.

- A believer with the motivational gift of exhortation, functioning in the five-fold ministry of evangelist, empowered by manifestation gifts of faith and prophecy.

These integrated patterns create distinctly assigned "fingerprints" that reflect God's intentional design. No combination is inherently superior to others; each serves essential Kingdom purposes. The Body requires this diversity for complete functionality.

When all three gift dimensions align under heaven's design, you enter the sweet spot of purpose where labor becomes rest and influence flows without striving. But when one layer is missing or misunderstood, the result is often misalignment:

- If you don't understand your motivational gifts, you may serve from obligation rather than design, leading to exhaustion and confusion about your purpose.

- If you never step into your ministry function, your God-given motivation remains private, limiting your impact and stalling your leadership.

- If you neglect the manifestation gifts, you end up relying on human effort rather than supernatural empowerment, which restricts what God can accomplish through you.

Consider Esther again. Her mercy motivation (heart), aligned with her queenly apostolic office (hands) and empowered by supernatural wisdom and favor (power), saved a nation. This integration wasn't accidental but divinely orchestrated, just as yours has been.

The Father has strategically positioned His daughters across every domain of influence—government, business, education, arts, media, family, and religion. Your Sacred Identity™ Signature Gift Set contains the precise configuration needed for your specific sphere. You are a sent one, commissioned with heaven's authority to transform culture, not just attend church. Both ministry and marketplace are longing for women who operate in their full, Spirit-led capacity.

CHAPTER 24

GIFT DISCOVERY AND DISCERNMENT

Create a reflective environment with your Bible, journal, and uninterrupted time. Begin with worship that focuses on God as Designer and Equipper.

Read 1 Corinthians 12:4–7 slowly three times. After each reading, pause to consider how the Trinity works together in distributing diverse gifts while maintaining unity of purpose. Journal your insights.

Here's one way to see it:

- The Father designs you (Psalm 139:13–14)
- The Son sends you (Ephesians 4:11)
- The Holy Spirit empowers you (1 Corinthians 12:11)

Let this truth sink in. You are the intentional work of a collaborative God who not only formed you, but now flows through you.

On a blank page, create three columns labeled "Motivational," "Ministry Five-Fold," and "Manifestation." Under each column, list the specific gifts within that category that consistently manifest in your life and ministry.

PRAY: *"Father, show me how these gifts are designed to work together as a unified expression of Your purpose through my life. Reveal the unique ministry fingerprint You've given me. Help me see beyond isolated gifts to the integrated design You've created."*

Ask these specific questions and journal what you receive:

- Which motivational gift forms my foundation and colors how I see needs?
- Which five-fold function best describes how I equip others?
- Which manifestation gifts consistently flow through my life?
- When my motivational, five-fold, and manifestation gifts align, what kind of ministry naturally flows out of me?" (Mentoring, building, nurturing, teaching, leading, etc.)
- Which area of culture do I feel most called to influence— business, education, family, media, government, the arts, or ministry?

Don't overthink these questions. You're not being tested, you're being revealed.

This may be the first time you've ever looked at your gift mix this way, and that's okay. Go slow. Sit with it. Even if your answers feel fuzzy at first, the goal here is clarity over perfection.

By the end, you'll be able to write a personal declaration that reflects your unique ministry design—and that's a powerful breakthrough.

If you're feeling stuck, distracted, unsure, or just want confirmation from someone who's walked this path and has helped hundreds of women of God pinpoint their Sacred Identity™, scan the QR code below.

You are not behind. You are becoming.

*To learn more or begin the experience, scan the QR code or visit **TheSacredBusiness.com** to access your* Sacred Identity™ Signature Gift Set.

"During the workshop, I realized I'd been hiding—not because I was afraid, but because I didn't fully understand who I was. Now that I have language for my leadership, I feel like I've been given permission to live it out. I'm leaving here with a clearer sense of identity—and something definitely has shifted."

— I. Roland, Workshop Attendee,
Sacred Identity™ Teaching

CHAPTER 25

FROM DISCOVERY TO DEPLOYMENT

Now that you've identified gifts, what's next? The goal isn't simply to admire them like trophies on a shelf, but to put them to work. Gifts grow by usage. Like muscles, they strengthen when exercised.

Think of David. He discovered a leadership and worship gift early (writing psalms, leading men in the wilderness). But it was years of using those gifts in caves and fields that prepared him to use them on the throne. Or think of someone with a gift of teaching; she might start by leading a small Bible study before speaking to hundreds. Faithfulness in small outlets often leads to greater ones.

So, start where you are. Is your gift leadership? Volunteer to organize something at church or work. Is it mercy? Serve in outreach or befriend someone who's hurting. Teaching? Offer to lead a small group or write devotions online. Prophecy? Spend extra time in prayer listening for God's words for people, and share with humility and love. Don't wait for a stage; use the gift in front of you.

As a sent one to the marketplaces of influence, recognize that your gifting operates differently in various contexts while maintaining its essential nature. The prophetic gift might manifest as strategic foresight in business settings. The pastoral gift might function as exceptional team leadership in corporate environments. The teaching gift might express as innovative training development in educational systems. Your Sacred ID remains constant while its expression adapts to specific cultural contexts.

A couple of years ago, I found myself in one of those in-between places—in transition but not quite there yet. In fact, the Lord showed me a vision of my transition as I was flying to Orlando for Apostle Joshua Giles' Joseph Summit. The weather was rough, and the actual flight was turbulent. But in the spirit, it felt like more than just bad skies. It felt like many of us on that plane were waiting on a supernatural tarmac, not just to lift off, but to launch out. It was as if we were all stalled in a holding pattern, waiting for the storm to lift so we could step fully into destiny.

Our actual flight landed later than expected, and I didn't even have time to change before going straight into the service. But it didn't matter, because hundreds of folks looked like they had just come through their own storm. None of us wanted to miss what God had planned. In the hallways, the restrooms, the arena, prophetic words were coming towards me fast: "Judge Deborah, what are you waiting for?" "Prophetic Innovator, Heaven and Earth are calling you!"

And yet the most powerful moment came on the return flight. People were tired, grumpy, worn down by the travel and the wait. But as we descended, something supernaturally shifted. Strangers started helping one another with luggage. Smiles returned. Bags were lifted. Grace flowed.

And in the spirit, I saw it clearly: we were being deployed. Each of us was parachuting back down to our neighborhoods, workplaces, and regions with Kingdom orders in hand—ambassadors carrying Heaven's greeting to Earth. In the spirit, some nodded with prayer hands. Some gave a quiet thumbs up. It wasn't just a plane ride, it was a prophetic dispatch. I knew in my spirit this is what it looks like when the called become the commissioned.

And like any commissioned soldier, your next move is preparation. Seek training and impartation. If you identify a certain gift strongly, surround yourself with mature Christians who operate in that gift. If you have a pastoral heart, maybe serve alongside a seasoned pastor to learn. If evangelism burns in you, go out witnessing with an evangelist. Gifts can be sharpened by mentorship and practice.

Remember that the Holy Spirit is the gift-giver, and He remains the gift-Enabler. Stay connected to Him. Keep your character growing to sustain your gifts. It's tragic when gifted individuals fall because their charisma took them where their character couldn't keep them. Avoid that trap by staying rooted in prayer, Scripture, and accountability.

And one more thing: enjoy the journey.

Discovering and using your gifts is meant to be deeply fulfilling. Eric Liddell, the Olympic runner and missionary, once said, "When I run, I feel His pleasure." That's what it's like operating in your gift. You feel God's pleasure because you're doing what He created you to do. There is joy and ease (even amid hard work) that accompanies flowing in your anointing.

CHAPTER 26

FROM ACTIVATION TO MULTIPLICATION

The ultimate purpose of spiritual gifts extends beyond personal expression to community multiplication. In the Kingdom economy, gifts reach maturity when they reproduce in others. Jesus modeled this progression perfectly. His ministry began with personal operation of gifts, developed through team demonstration, and culminated in releasing disciples to operate in these same gifts.

Paul captured this multiplication mandate when instructing Timothy to entrust his learning "to reliable people who will also be qualified to teach others" (2 Timothy 2:2). This verse outlines a four-generation reproduction chain: Paul → Timothy → Reliable People → Others. This pattern reveals that gift maturity involves not just personal mastery but generational transfer.

Throughout church history, movements that sustained long-term impact created systematic gift multiplication pathways. As we saw in earlier chapters, the Moravian prayer community designed intentional mentoring structures where seasoned intercessors guided emerging gift carriers. John Wesley's Methodist class meeting system created progressive leadership development, ensuring gift reproduction across generations. Modern disciple-making movements establish deliberate generational growth, ensuring gifts multiply rather than concentrate in founding leaders.

Your gifts were never meant to terminate with you but to transfer through you. The measure of your gift stewardship isn't just how effectively you operate in them but how successfully you replicate them in others.

SACRED PRAYER: *"Heavenly Father, I recognize that the gifts You've entrusted to me were never meant to terminate with me. I commit to being not just a practitioner but a multiplier. I release any unhealthy ownership of these gifts and embrace my responsibility to reproduce them in others. Give me wisdom to identify, patience to develop, and courage to release emerging gift carriers. May what You've invested in me multiply through generations of faithful stewards, creating exponential Kingdom impact. In Jesus' name, Amen."*

Schedule a meaningful conversation with at least one person you've identified, with the intentional purpose of affirming and activating their similar gifting. Share what you've observed about their potential, suggest a few growth opportunities, and commit to walking alongside them as you both continue to grow in your gift journey.

CHAPTER 27

THE COVENANT OF CONFIRMATION

Throughout Scripture, we see a consistent pattern: When believers step out in faith-filled obedience, God confirms their steps with supernatural validation. Mark 16:20 describes this divine partnership: "Then the disciples went out and preached everywhere, and the Lord worked with them and confirmed his word by the signs that accompanied it."

This wasn't exceptional—it was expected. Divine confirmation often follows Spirit-led action.

Moses is a perfect example. He didn't stride into his calling with full confidence, he trembled. Questioned. Hesitated. "What if they don't believe me?" he asked. But even in his uncertainty, he obeyed. And it was in that obedience that God responded with signs: a staff that turned into a serpent, a hand made leprous then whole again, water turned to blood. Each sign wasn't just supernatural, it was deeply personal. God was saying, "I'm with you. Keep going."

Gideon, too, needed reassurance. He wasn't trying to test God in rebellion, but in humility. And God met him with patience, confirming his call not once, but repeatedly. First through fire on the altar. Then through the fleece. Then through a dream overheard in the enemy's camp. Heaven echoed Gideon's assignment until the man who once hid in a winepress rose as a deliverer.

The early church witnessed this covenant of confirmation constantly. As they preached, prayed, healed, and served, God backed their boldness with supernatural results. The gospel wasn't just explained; it was demonstrated through power.

This covenant of confirmation remains active today. When you step out in faithful stewardship of your gifts, God promises to partner with you. It may not always come in dramatic ways or immediate outcomes, but make no mistake, He still confirms what He commissions.

Here are some of the ways confirmation might show up on your journey—not as a checklist to chase, but as evidence of God's ongoing partnership:

You may encounter supernatural manifestations—moments when healing breaks forth, prophetic words are confirmed, miracles occur, or divine insight flows with accuracy and authority. These aren't about performance; they are signs God is near and involved in your assignment.

At other times, there's simply an internal witness—a deep, Spirit-led peace that settles in your spirit, affirming, "This is right. This is God." Even when the full picture isn't clear, your spirit resonates with alignment.

Confirmation also shows up through external fruit. When lives are changed, healing happens, or others are drawn to Jesus through your gift, that fruit speaks loudly. Transformation is one of the clearest signs that God is breathing on what you're doing.

Then there's corporate affirmation. Trusted mentors, mature believers, or spiritual leaders may recognize and call out the grace operating in you—often confirming what you've already sensed privately.

And sometimes, confirmation comes through providential arrangement. A door opens at just the right time. A conversation aligns precisely with your prayer. A resource shows up before you even knew you needed it. These moments carry God's fingerprint—they are too specific to be coincidence.

Remember, these confirmations don't create your calling or establish your gift. That was already settled in Heaven by the Giver. What they do is affirm the timing, readiness, and alignment of how that gift is meant to function right now. You were never meant to hide what God invested in you. As Jesus taught in the parable of the talents (Matthew 25:14–30), the master was pleased with the servants who multiplied their talents and displeased with the one who buried his in fear. No burying here, Divine Daughter of God—we are going to invest what He gave us.

Perhaps an opportunity is already before you, something that has been tugging at your heart. It might scare you a bit (often a sign it's God, because it requires faith!). Take that step. Even if it's small, God can steer a moving ship better than one still in the harbor. Start moving in the direction He's prompting.

And know that as you activate your gifts, Heaven will back you up. The Lord partners with us in our obedience. Just as He confirmed the preaching of the disciples with signs following (Mark 16:20), He will confirm your obedient use of gifts with fruit and grace following.

CHAPTER 28

FINAL COMMISSIONING: FROM REVELATION TO REVOLUTION

Divine, you stand at a prophetic threshold. The journey from identity to gift discovery now transitions to activation and impact. What God has worked in you will now work through you. The private revelation becomes public revolution as Heaven's investment generates Kingdom return.

This moment carries both profound responsibility and exhilarating privilege. You steward gifts that angels long to understand. You carry capacity to manifest Heaven's reality in earthly contexts. You participate in the ongoing ministry of Christ Himself through His Body.

Let this truth settle deep: You are not simply operating your gifts; you are yielding your vessel for the gifter Himself to operate through you. Your gifts aren't tools you master, but conduits through which the Master flows. This perspective replaces performance pressure with yielded partnership.

Now, rise in the authority of your calling. Build what Heaven assigned you to build. Release what God entrusted you to release. Your gifts have assignments attached. The world awaits the manifestation of what God has cultivated in secret.

"For we are God's handiwork, created in Christ Jesus to do good works, which God prepared in advance for us to do" (Ephesians 2:10).

Your gifts are God's preparation. Your activation is God's pleasure. Your impact is God's purpose.

Step fully into all He's prepared for you.

CHAPTER 29

SACRED IDENTITY INVITATION

Beloved, the journey of discovering your Sacred ID is both profound and practical. While the framework has been introduced, your personal discovery journey still awaits.

That's why I created The Sacred Identity™ Signature Gift Set—a guided, three-part prophetic experience designed to walk you through your unique gifting, wiring, and Heaven-sent assignments.

Women from all walks of life have encountered breakthrough through this journey—like one beloved sister who faithfully served under a renowned prophetic ministry for years. Out of deep admiration, she eventually adopted the title of the prophet she once supported, genuinely desiring to honor the legacy she had helped build. But in the quiet tension between obedience and expectation, it became clear: her lead gift wasn't prophecy, but *serving*—a grace often overlooked but richly anointed. Rather than being a platform to perform, her gift was designed as a foundation to sustain. And like so many others, she had unknowingly traded the power of alignment for the pressure of imitation. Her story reminds us how vital it is to know—not guess—how Heaven has wired us to function.

Then there's Monique, who once believed her highest contribution was serving faithfully behind the scenes—singing, supporting, and showing up. But clarity changed everything. Her Sacred Identity™ revealed a leader's heart long buried under humility. Now, she isn't just echoing vision, she's casting it. And she's doing it with strategy, strength, and spiritual precision.

....

> *"When you don't know your divine assignment, it's easy to borrow someone else's title—and miss your own oil."*
>
> —Tia Brewer-Footman

....

After introducing this framework at a conference, one woman told me, "I can't stop talking about this—I even told my girlfriends!" Another asked if I could bring the Sacred Identity™ experience to her church. "I want to give every member an assessment," she said. Yet another leaned in and asked with such hunger, "How can I go deeper into this?" These weren't casual compliments. They were confirmations. Heaven is stirring something in the daughters of God—and Sacred Identity™ is the key they've been waiting for.

Through this experience, you won't just learn about your gifts in isolation—you'll start to see the divine pattern that emerges when your gifts come into agreement with Heaven's intention for your life.

The Sacred Identity™ Signature Gift Set includes:

- A self-paced **assessment** to help you identify your unique mix of motivational, ministry, and manifestation gifts

- A **step-by-step training experience** to walk you through your results with clarity and prophetic insight

- A **supportive reflection and activation guide** to help you process what God reveals along the way

- Access to a **private community** of like-hearted believers who are journeying through this discovery with you

The Signature Gift Set was prayerfully designed to mentor you through the process so you're not wandering alone or left to assemble the pieces by yourself.

This is more than a tool. It's a *witness* of who you really are, and what God is building in and through you.

*To learn more or begin the experience, scan the QR code or visit **TheSacredBusiness.com** to access your Sacred Identity™ Signature Gift Set.*

FINAL WORDS

Divine, you have labored through deep waters—confronting false names, receiving Heaven's true blueprint, and awakening to the grace God uniquely placed within you.

Your Sacred Identity™ is not just a revelation. It's a responsibility.

And now that you've glimpsed what's possible, don't stop here.

Don't go back to guessing. Don't return to patching your purpose together from well-meaning voices, online quizzes, or borrowed callings. You are not random. You are not overlooked. You are not optional to the Kingdom plan.

Heaven has been waiting for your agreement.

So if you haven't yet, take the next step. The Sacred Identity™ Signature Gift Set was created to guide you deeper, because this part of your journey is too precious to piece together alone.

But this is not the end.

In the chapters ahead, we'll go beyond personal clarity into divine commissioning. You'll see why your gifts were never meant to stay tucked inside a personality profile or reserved for safe stages and side hustles.

They were always meant to build something greater.

This next stretch of the journey is about **legacy** and the Kingdom impact your gifts were born to release.

So breathe deep.
Say yes again.
And keep going.
Your name is known. Your gifts are needed.
And your time is now.

Your Gift
Is Not a
Side Hustle

CHAPTER 30

YOU ARE NOT FOR SALE

Your gift is not a product. It's a prophecy.

And while the world may try to package it, promote it, monetize it, or water it down, what Heaven placed in you is far too sacred to be reduced to a commodity. You are not for sale.

There's a growing pressure—especially for women of faith in visible roles—to perform their gift instead of minister their gift. The difference? Performance seeks applause and profit; ministry seeks purpose and God's pleasure.

Let's be clear: There is nothing wrong with profiting from your gifts when done in alignment with Heaven's intent. In fact, impact and income are meant to walk together when stewarded righteously. What we must reject is the pressure to pimp out our anointing for validation or platform, forgetting the sacred reason we were entrusted with power in the first place.

As Dr. Myles Munroe once said, "When the purpose of a thing is not known, abuse is inevitable." If we lose sight of why God gave us our gifts, we risk misusing them, not always through evil intentions, but through unexamined motives. We may begin chasing income or influence and call it ministry when it's really self-promotion dressed in spiritual language.

But God is bringing a holy recalibration. The Holy Spirit is purifying our posture, not to keep us small, but to keep us aligned. Remember, we were not anointed to make a name for ourselves; we were anointed to glorify His name.

You are not a product to be marketed to the highest bidder. You are a vessel of glory, and when you walk in obedience, your gifts will bear both fruit and provision.

You weren't anointed to sell yourself. You were chosen to serve with power.

CHAPTER 31

THE MARKETPLACE VS. THE KINGDOM

Divine, there is a stark difference between marketplace mentality and Kingdom stewardship.

The marketplace says, "Package yourself, polish your brand, maximize profit margins." The Kingdom says: "Surrender yourself, refine your character, multiply eternal impact."

Let me speak with tender directness. You live in a culture that commodifies everything—even spirituality. And while platforms and profit are not evil in themselves, they require intentional alignment. Social media has trained even sincere believers to think in terms of metrics rather than ministry. The algorithms reward what's marketable, not necessarily what's meaningful. If you're not prayerfully anchored, you'll find yourself shifting from stewarding a divine gift to simply selling a polished product.

As someone who understands this world both spiritually and professionally, I get it.

At the highest levels, I've represented media, marketing, finance, and government as a former television news anchor turned Sacred Brand Strategist and advisor to Fortune 100 companies and faith-based institutions. With a Bachelor's degree in Mass Communications and a Master's degree in Brand Communications (graduating with honors and a smile), I've trained and mentored hundreds of seasoned and emerging leaders, creators, and communicators, and I've stood on platforms beside generals in the faith.

So hear me clearly when I say there's nothing wrong with packaging, positioning, or profit when it's done in alignment with God's voice, God's timing, and God's intention. You can honor your calling and receive compensation. You can build a brand and stay pure in heart. You can be both anointed and excellent, as long as you're anchored in the One who called you.

What we must reject is the temptation to perform our calling to fit trends or prostitute our gift to the cultural auction block. You were never meant to be pimped out by the pressures of visibility, nor exploited by the expectations of culture. You were sent—not sold.

This isn't about rejecting platforms or influence. This is about reclaiming the posture of your heart. Yes, your gift may generate income, and it should when stewarded God's way. But the gift was never meant to be for sale. "Freely you have received; freely give" (Matthew 10:8). That doesn't mean you charge nothing, it means your values are never up for negotiation.

Consider Bezalel from Exodus 31:1–5. God said: "See, I have chosen Bezalel ... and I have filled him with the Spirit of God, with wisdom, with understanding, with knowledge and with all kinds of skills—to make artistic designs ... and engage in all kinds of crafts."

Bezalel was a craftsman, a marketplace man, yet God said he was filled with the Spirit. His work was sacred because his heart was surrendered. His creativity wasn't for consumption. It was an assignment.

Maybe you started with pure intentions. But somewhere along the way, your fruit started being measured by followers, not faithfulness. It's time to recalibrate.

Remember Simon the sorcerer? He tried to buy the Holy Spirit's power from Peter. Peter's rebuke was sharp: "May your money perish with you ..." (Acts 8:20).

The gifts of God are not merchandise. They're a trust.

Your calling is not a side gig. It's a sacred assignment. Honor it, and God will take care of the rest (including the provision).

CHAPTER 32

THE TENT-MAKING MODEL: KINGDOM PROVISION

Perhaps you're thinking, "But I need to earn a living. Is it wrong to receive payment for my gift?" Not at all.

Consider Priscilla and Aquila, a faithful married couple who crafted tents by trade, yet also carried deep spiritual authority. They worked alongside Paul to support themselves financially, while also discipling Apollos and hosting churches in their home (Acts 18:1–3; Romans 16:3–5). Their lives demonstrate that provision and purpose can coexist without competition.

The tent-making supported their living; the gospel was their life. The distinction is critical.

Some of you will be called to full-time ministry, where your gift and your livelihood are one and the same. Others will be called to marketplace influence, where your gift operates powerfully while you earn elsewhere. Still others will walk a hybrid path, where your gift generates some income while remaining unburdened by financial pressure. None of these paths is more spiritual than the others.

What matters is your heart posture and your obedience to your specific assignment.

This model still plays out today. Many modern-day Kingdom leaders live this divine tension—bi-vocational pastors, worship leaders who run businesses, creatives who consult by day and minister by night. Provision doesn't compete with purpose when obedience is the goal.

Queen Esther held governmental position and authority—a prestigious role that provided her with wealth and status. Yet when the moment of divine purpose arrived, she was ready to risk it all: "If I perish, I perish" (Esther 4:16). Her position was the platform; her purpose was the preservation of God's people. The role financed her life; her calling defined her legacy.

SACRED EXERCISE

Which model is God calling you to in this season: full-time ministry, marketplace influence, or the hybrid path? How does knowing this model free you from comparison with others walking different assignments?

SACRED PRAYER | *Father of Wisdom, I thank You for each Divine daughter reading these words. You've crafted unique economic models for each one's calling—some to be supported fully by their gift, others to support their gift through other means, and many to walk an annointed middle path. I release* *clarity over their financial stewardship model and break off all comparison, confusion, and corruption that has clouded their vision. Let them see their provision path with crystal clarity, that they may walk unburdened by either poverty or profit-centered thinking. In Jesus' name, Amen.*

CHAPTER 33

WHEN GIFTING BECOMES GRINDING

It starts subtly.

You say yes a few too many times. You stretch yourself a little further than grace allows. You serve, pour, lead, give, encourage, until the very thing that once felt sacred now feels suffocating.

This is what happens when gifting becomes grinding.

The gift hasn't left you. The anointing is still real. But the weight of expectation, especially self-imposed or culture-fed, can crush the joy out of what God called holy. And because we're spiritual, we push through it. We quote Scripture over it. We try to "pray it away." But what we need isn't more pressure. It's a pause.

THE HUSTLE DECEPTION

Beloved, there's a deception sweeping through Kingdom work—a glorification of hustle, an elevation of exhaustion as some badge of honor. "Look how busy I am for Jesus" has become the modern martyrdom. But I must tell you plainly: burnout is not a fruit of the Spirit; exhaustion is not evidence of faithfulness.

This hustle mentality has infiltrated ministry through marketplace teachings that, while perhaps effective for building businesses, can be devastating for building Kingdom. Behind many of these teachings lurks a spirit of Mammon—not just money itself, but the love and pursuit of it as primary motivation.

Jesus warned us we cannot serve both God and Mammon (Matthew 6:24). When hustle becomes your driver, you've unwittingly shifted masters. The evidence appears in your relationships, your health, your spiritual life—all sacrificed on the altar of "more."

Burnout doesn't always come from sin. Sometimes it comes from stewardship without boundaries, ministry without margin, helping without Heaven's green light.

The prophet Elijah, after his greatest victory on Mount Carmel, collapsed into exhaustion and depression under a broom tree (1 Kings 19:4-5). This wasn't because he lacked faith or anointing, it was because supernatural expenditure requires supernatural renewal. Even Jesus withdrew regularly to lonely places to pray, refusing to let the demands of ministry override His communion with the Father (Luke 5:16).

You can't sustain what you haven't surrendered. And you can't steward well what you're afraid to rest.

THE PRODUCTION TRAP

The enemy of spirit-led flow is forced output.

Our culture worships productivity. We measure worth by what we produce, how quickly we produce it, and how much of it we can generate. This mindset has crept into ministry, creating constant pressure to produce sermons, books, posts, programs, and events, often without the holy gestation period such births require.

Recall how God instructed Moses to speak to the rock to bring forth water, but in his frustration, Moses struck it instead (Numbers 20:7-12). He produced the result (water flowed), but he missed the process God prescribed. The consequence was severe—Moses forfeited his opportunity to enter the Promised Land.

This serves as a sober warning. Producing results through methods other than those God ordained can cost us our inheritance, even if those methods appear successful by external measures.

Here are some signs you've shifted into grinding mode:

- You start resenting the very opportunities you prayed for.
- You equate busyness with purpose.
- You feel guilty for resting.
- You struggle to hear God clearly because your capacity is flooded.
- Your creativity has been replaced by copycat formulas.
- You're more focused on output than encounter.
- Your ministry vocabulary includes "must," "should," and "have to" more than "get to," "blessed to," and "invited to."

This is not selfishness—it's spiritual stewardship. You weren't built to manufacture spiritual fruit; you were designed to abide and let it grow.

Jesus said, "I am the vine, you are the branches. If you remain in Me ... you will bear much fruit; apart from Me you can do nothing" (John 15:5). We quote that, yet how often do we run off trying to do something apart from Him? The result is frustration, emptiness, and sometimes collapse.

If you find yourself in grind mode, here's Heaven's invitation: Come back to the Source. Your gift is most powerful when yielded, not when hyped.

THE RHYTHM OF CREATION

Let's learn from the Master Creator Himself. In Genesis 1, we see God's creative process unfold in a rhythm of work and evaluation: "God saw that it was good." He didn't rush from creating fish to creating animals. He paused, evaluated, and affirmed each day's work before moving to the next.

And what did the Creator do on the seventh day? He rested. Not because He was tired, but because He was establishing a pattern for all creation to follow. Rest isn't just recovery from work; it's an essential part of the creative process itself.

Your gift flows from this same divine nature. It requires rhythm—the inhale of receiving, the exhale of releasing. When you operate solely in exhale mode—constantly outputting without inhaling fresh inspiration—you're functioning at half capacity.

Mary of Bethany understood this rhythm. While Martha rushed about in service preparation, Mary sat at Jesus' feet, receiving. When Jesus affirmed that Mary had "chosen the better part" (Luke 10:42), He wasn't diminishing service; He was establishing priority: receiving must precede giving.

Later, it was Mary who anointed Jesus with costly perfume (John 12:3)—an extravagant act of ministry that Jesus said would be remembered wherever the gospel is preached. Her ability to minister powerfully flowed directly from her prioritization of being with Jesus before doing for Jesus.

SACRED EXERCISE

In what ways have you been functioning in constant "exhale" mode without the consecrated inhale of receiving from God? What specific activities or commitments keep you in production mode without renewal?

SACRED PRAYER | *Divine Orchestrator, You created the cosmos in perfect rhythm and designed us to function in that same cadence of receiving and releasing. I speak alignment over each daughter's internal clock—breaking the tyranny of constant production and establishing Heaven's rhythm in her ministry. Release her from the addiction to achievement and the idol of impact. Restore her to the sweet synchronicity of abiding and bearing, waiting and moving, being and doing. Let her gift flow from encounter, not effort. In Jesus' name, Amen.*

CHAPTER 34

SACRED REST FOR SACRED WORK

Sometimes the most spiritual thing you can do for your gift is to rest. Step away from the stage or the sermon or the emails or the content calendar and recalibrate with Jesus. Let Him remind you that you are a daughter before you are a leader. Let Him minister to the parts of you that have become dry or mechanized.

THE THEOLOGY OF REST

There exists a profound theology of rest that much of Western Christianity has neglected. Hebrews 4:9-11 declares, "There remains, then, a Sabbath-rest for the people of God; for anyone who enters God's rest also rests from their works, just as God did from his. Let us, therefore, make every effort to enter that rest ..."

Notice the paradox: We must "make every effort" to enter rest. This isn't passive, it's deliberate. Rest is not something that happens to you when you collapse; it's a spiritual posture you cultivate intentionally.

When Elijah burned out after great exploits, God's remedy was food and sleep, *then* a gentle whisper of direction (1 Kings 19). The Lord restored the man before assigning the next mission.

Your gift is divine, but you are human. You need rhythms of renewal. Don't fear that stepping back will mean losing momentum. In God's Kingdom, sometimes we must "come aside" (Mark 6:31) to a quiet place so that when we return, we carry greater power.

RESTING IS STRATEGIC, NOT LAZY

Let me speak against a lie that has taken root: Rest is not laziness; it's strategy. In our productivity-obsessed culture, rest feels like failure. But in Kingdom economy, rest is fertile ground for revelation.

Consider Jacob's dream at Bethel (Genesis 28:10-22). It was while he slept that he saw the ladder to Heaven with angels ascending and descending. He didn't strive for this encounter; it came to him in rest. Some of your most significant breakthroughs, creative downloads, and strategic insights will come not while grinding, but while resting in God's presence. Not to lighten the seriousness of the matter, but why do I get a ton of my revelation while brushing my teeth? Apparently, Heaven isn't just into healing—it's into hygiene too. But in all seriousness, even Jesus often withdrew to lonely places despite constant demands (Luke 5:15–16). This wasn't procrastination, it was prioritization. He knew that communion with the Father was the wellspring from which His ministry flowed. His example shatters our idolatry of busyness.

As you learn to rest and abide, something beautiful happens: Your gift starts flowing again. Not from striving, but from the overflow of the Spirit. Ideas come effortlessly during a walk in nature that never came under fluorescent office lights at 10:00 p.m. Messages download in your spirit in the secret place that a week of staring at a screen couldn't produce.

God breathes on what is yielded. He multiplies what is consecrated. He will propel your ministry or project further in one Holy Spirit moment than you could in a year of grinding on your own.

DIFFERENT KINDS OF REST

Kingdom rest isn't one-dimensional. Inspired in part by the brilliant work of Dr. Saundra Dalton-Smith in *Sacred Rest*, which outlines seven distinct types of rest, this list builds upon her framework through the lens of your divine identity, anchoring each rest type in Scripture and applying it to the unique rhythms of purpose-driven women of faith.

1. **Sabbath Rest**
   The rest that reminds you you're not the source—God is.
   Regular, rhythmic ceasing that anchors you in God's sovereignty, not your striving (Exodus 20:8–11).

2. **Spiritual Rest**
   The rest that frees you from performing and returns you to Presence.
   Soul-deep restoration found in Christ's finished work and your union with Him (Matthew 11:28–30).

3. **Creative Rest**

   The rest that reignites your vision by letting beauty minister to your spirit.

   For builders and creators, it's the sacred pause where inspiration is refilled (Leviticus 25:4).

4. **Physical Rest**

   The rest that honors your humanity and restores your body for divine assignment.

   Sleep, nourishment, and stillness are not weaknesses—they're fuel for obedience (1 Kings 19:5–8).

5. **Mental Rest**

   The rest that quiets overthinking so you can receive divine strategy.

   Stepping back from constant problem-solving to make space for peace and clarity (Philippians 4:6–7).

6. **Relational Rest**

   The rest that comes from being seen, safe, and supported in sacred community.

   Choosing connections that replenish rather than drain your spirit (Proverbs 13:20; Mark 3:16).

7. **Sensory Rest**

   The rest that silences the noise so you can hear God's whisper.

   Unplugging from overstimulation to tune into the stillness of His voice (Psalm 46:10).

SACRED EXERCISE

Which of these seven types of rest do you most desperately need in this season? What practical steps can you take this week to begin restoring that dimension?

SACRED PRAYER | *Lord of the Sabbath, I thank You for each daughter who has stewarded gifts with faithfulness but now needs renewal. I release divine permission over them to enter Your rest without guilt or fear. Break the chains of performance that have convinced them that worth comes from work. Restore their souls beside still waters. Show them that in Your Kingdom, power flows from peace, not pressure. Let them discover their greatest breakthroughs await them not in striving but in surrendering to sacred rest. In Jesus' name, Amen.*

CHAPTER 35

PURIFY AND REFOCUS

You've rested. You've returned. Now it's time to realign your heart.

Sacred rest softens us to hear again—clearing the noise so we can discern what's been fueling our gift. And sometimes, what's revealed is not all glory. As you step back into motion, this chapter invites you to examine your motives with the same intentionality you gave to your rhythms. Because flow without purity is still misalignment.

Let's return to the heart. Why did you start? Why did you answer God's call to begin with? Likely it was something pure—love for God, compassion for people, a desire to make a difference. That's your "why." We must guard it fiercely.

If you suspect that any corrupt motivations have tangled into your gift (and for most of us, at times, they do), simply bring them to Jesus. He already knows. Confess, "Lord, I've let pride (or greed, or insecurity, or competition) get in here. Cleanse me. Renew my perspective." He will. He loves when we come to Him for refinement.

Let's walk through a few of the common ways pure motives can become compromised:

Sometimes it begins with **validation-seeking**—using your gift to prove your worth rather than fulfill your purpose. It often wears the mask of excellence, but when criticism crushes you, the root is revealed.

Or maybe it's **comparison**—measuring your gift expression against someone else's instead of the standard of your unique assignment. This either inflates pride or sinks you into despair.

Control can also creep in—manifesting as micromanaging, over-working, or an inability to release. It's when we try to manufacture outcomes instead of trusting God's process.

You might notice **people-pleasing** taking over—reshaping your voice, message, or boundaries to gain approval rather than fulfilling the assignment Heaven gave you.

There's also the subtle influence of **financial idolatry**—prioritizing income over Spirit-led conviction. When profit drives decisions more than conviction, it distorts the flow.

Then there's **platform addiction**—when visibility becomes more important than purity. Jealousy, hustle, and performance often trail behind this one.

And finally, **orphan mentality**—operating from a mindset of scarcity rather than secure sonship. It shows up in hoarding opportunities, withholding collaboration, and fearing you'll be forgotten.

These aren't just attitude issues—they're heart postures that need recalibration.

Nehemiah faced opposition while rebuilding Jerusalem's walls. His enemies invited him to come down from the wall to meet them, but he replied: "I am carrying on a great project and cannot go down. Why should the work stop while I leave it and go down to you?" (Nehemiah 6:3). This exemplifies purity of focus—he recognized distractions designed to derail his divine assignment.

Sometimes, practically, this may mean a season of serving in obscurity again to get our hearts right. Or it may mean giving something away for no cost when we sense we've grown too transactional. Listen to the Holy Spirit. He will show you what detox your heart might need.

I've seen this in the lives of Kingdom builders across different spaces.

Like the Christian entrepreneur who, whenever he senses money creeping into the wrong place in his heart, will intentionally give away some of his best content—not out of obligation, but as a spiritual reset. It's his way of saying, "God, You're still Lord over this."

Or the worship leader who notices performance and gigging creeping in and begins showing up again in small, unannounced prayer rooms just to pour out before the Lord without lights, cameras, or applause. To remember it's still about Presence, not platform.

I've lived this too. As a brand strategist and builder who teaches women how to platform their calling, I've had moments where God nudged me to pause—to fast before a launch, to refine an offer I was excited about, or to wait until my posture was aligned with Heaven's pace. Divine resets aren't setbacks. They're realignments.

These are the kinds of rhythms that keep our gifting pure and our impact sustainable.

Because at the end of the day, I'm not just guiding women of God to build brands. We're building altars.

THE CLEANSING OF THE TEMPLE

Remember Jesus cleansing the temple? He flipped tables because merchants had turned a holy place into a marketplace (Matthew 21:12-13). Sometimes the Holy Spirit may need to flip a few tables in our hearts—overturning the hustle, the self-promotion—to restore His house of prayer within us. Welcome His refining. It's never to harm you, it's to restore you.

This cleansing is not punishment, it's purification. It's Jesus protecting the consecrated purpose of your gift from commercial contamination. When He overturns tables in your ministry, thank Him. He's preserving your legacy.

You'll find on the other side of that cleansing a fresh anointing. When the impurities are skimmed off gold, the gold shines more brilliantly. Your gift will shine more purely after you let God refine your motives.

RECALIBRATING TO FIRST LOVE

Revelation 2:2-4 contains a sobering message to the church at Ephesus: "I know your deeds, your hard work and your perseverance ... Yet I hold this against you: You have forsaken the love you had at first."

This church was doctrinally sound, morally pure, and diligently working, yet they had lost their primary motivation: love for Jesus. They were doing the right things for the wrong reasons.

This passage speaks directly to gifted leaders whose ministries appear successful but whose hearts have drifted from their first love. The remedy? "Remember the height from which you have fallen! Repent and do the things you did at first" (Revelation 2:5).

What were those "first things" for you? For most, it was simple devotion—unhurried time in God's presence, worship without agenda, Scripture read for relationship rather than sermon material, prayer motivated by desire rather than duty.

Return to these first expressions. They will rekindle the purity that made your gift so powerful to begin with.

SACRED EXERCISE

Write down your original "why"—the pure motivation that first led you to step out in your gift. Then list ways you can recalibrate to that original purpose in this current season.

SACRED PRAYER | *Refiner's Fire, I invite You to examine the hearts of these Kingdom daughters. With tender precision, expose any corruption that has entangled their pure calling. Overturn the tables of self-promotion, validation-seeking, and financial idolatry. Restore the house of prayer within them. Let them feel Your zealous love protecting their purpose, not Your judgment condemning their missteps. Reignite their first love. Remind them of the pure joy that accompanied their original yes to You. Establish them once again in motivation so pure that the gift flows with fresh anointing, uncontaminated by the world's values. In Jesus' name, Amen.*

CHAPTER 36

FREELY RECEIVED, FREELY GIVE

Let's also talk about generosity. One way to keep a gift from becoming a mere product is to regularly use it in situations where there's no personal gain, simply to bless. If you're a speaker (ministry or marketplace) who usually gets paid, volunteer sometimes where no one knows you, just to serve. If you're a businesswoman with strategy gifts, mentor a younger woman for free. If you're an artist who sells work, occasionally create something and donate it or bless someone who can't afford it.

THE KINGDOM ECONOMICS OF GENEROSITY

When Jesus sent out the disciples, He instructed them, "Freely you have received; freely give" (Matthew 10:8). This principle establishes Kingdom economics: What flows without cost to you should flow, at times, without cost from you.

This doesn't mean you never receive payment for your gift; the Scripture also affirms "the worker deserves his wages" (1 Timothy

5:18). Rather, it establishes that generosity should punctuate your gift expression regularly.

Consider the Levitical law of gleaning (Leviticus 19:9-10), where farmers were instructed not to harvest the corners of their fields or pick up fallen grapes, leaving them instead for the foreigner and the poor. This wasn't optional charity, it was mandated generosity—built into their business model by divine design. We'll talk more about building sacred businesses in later chapters.

Similarly, your ministry or business should have "corners" deliberately left unharvested—areas where your gift operates purely for blessing, not for income. This builds divine economics and social justice into your model.

These acts of "freely giving" remind your soul the gift belongs to God. It keeps you grounded in the joy of why you do this. The irony is, such generosity often increases the oil on your gift, which in time brings more provision anyway. But you're not doing it for that— you're doing it to honor God and people.

THE MIRACLE OF MULTIPLICATION

Kingdom economics operate on multiplication, not mere addition. When the disciples faced five thousand hungry people, they presented Jesus with five loaves and two fish. His response is instructive: "Bring them here to Me" (Matthew 14:18). What happened next defies natural economics—Jesus blessed the food, broke it, and it multiplied beyond mathematical explanation.

The pattern is clear: Whatever we surrender to Jesus, He blesses. Whatever He blesses, He breaks. Whatever He breaks, He multiplies.

This applies directly to your gift. When you surrender it fully to Jesus (not using it primarily for self-advancement), He blesses it with His approval. Often, there follows a breaking—a season of testing, refining, or hiddenness that feels like reduction, not expansion. But after the breaking comes multiplication beyond what human effort could produce.

We see this in Joseph's life. His gift of leadership and administration was surrendered to God, blessed with favor, broken through betrayal and imprisonment, then multiplied into second-in-command over Egypt.

The multiplication phase often includes provision, but provision was never the primary goal—impact was.

Heaven's economy is different. When we give, we receive. When we refresh others, we are refreshed (Proverbs 11:25). Try it and watch God take care of you.

For example, when I would speak in the past, I often invited young girls or women to be my special front-row guests—especially those between blessings or still discovering their sense of purpose. Sometimes, instead of waiting for them to come to me, I would go to where they were, meeting them in their environment, listening, praying, and spending intentional time before leaving the city. These weren't just sweet moments. They were sacred seeds. They reminded me of the "why" behind the work and kept my gift anchored in service, not spotlight.

FROM ROOM SERVICE TO REAL SERVICE

I had just wrapped an assignment at the Arizona Biltmore the night before—a luxury resort known for hosting presidents, dignitaries, and the elite. The next morning, instead of enjoying a $75 room service breakfast, I felt the Spirit pressing on my heart. Just miles away from the elegance of the resort was a neighborhood with one of the highest rates of childhood hunger in the state—precious, predominantly Hispanic children facing food insecurity at rates higher than the national average. I couldn't sit in that luxury and ignore what God was stirring.

So I canceled my personal plans, called an Uber, and made my way to St. Mary's Food Bank. I spent the afternoon volunteering with their after-school program. The staff and children welcomed me with open arms. I toured the space, asked about their needs and goals, and offered to support however I could. But what happened before I left undid me. The children—bright, joy-filled, resilient—sang me a song they had made up in Spanish. They had learned my name was Tia and, knowing what it meant, breathed new life into it. *"Auntie."* They didn't just see a guest, they saw family. And in return, they gave me more than I could have ever given them. I left full—not from luxury, but from love.

THE MINISTRY OF MULTIPLICATION

Multiplication doesn't stop with outcomes; it continues through people. "The things you have heard from me...entrust to reliable people who will also be qualified to teach others" (2 Timothy 2:2). That's four generations in one command. Jesus modeled it: He didn't just perform miracles; He commissioned miracle-workers. He didn't just teach; He sent teachers. Your gift isn't meant to terminate with you—it's meant to reproduce.

SACRED EXERCISE

What "corners of your field" can you intentionally leave unharvested—areas where you regularly practice generosity with your gift without expectation of return? How can you build this into your ministry or business model?

Glad you asked... This is actually something I teach and walk out regularly in my own brand ecosystem. And if you're feeling stirred here — like you're ready to evolve from clarity into greater strategy — I have a whole training arm designed just for this.

It's called **The Sacred Brand Institute** — where I, along with a trusted team of Kingdom-minded women, help you activate and align your divine DNA into visible, sustainable impact. We walk alongside purpose-driven leaders like you, helping you build influence God's way, with a justice lens, marketplace clarity, and ministry purity.

There's a waitlist to join the next cohort and get up-to-date information on the next opening.

But more on that... later. Right now, just stay in this moment. Let the Holy Spirit finish what He started.

SACRED PRAYER | *God of Abundant Supply, I thank You for each generous-hearted daughter reading these words. Uproot all scarcity thinking that would cause her to clutch tightly what You've freely given. Establish divine economics in her ministry—strategic corners left for blessing without compensation. As she freely gives, supernaturally multiply both her impact and her provision. Break off orphan mindsets that hoard rather than release. Ignite in her a passion for multiplication, seeing her gift reproduced in generations beyond herself. Let her taste the joy of abundance that comes not through clutching but through releasing. In Jesus' name, Amen.*

CHAPTER 37

GUARD THE SACRED

Your gift is sacred. It's okay to set boundaries that protect its sacredness. For example, you might limit commercial use of your gift to what God specifically directs so you aren't constantly "selling" what should sometimes be just given. Or you might keep certain aspects of your gift purely in ministry context so you don't lose the wonder.

SACRED BOUNDARIES

In our boundary-challenged culture, many believers feel guilty for establishing limits around their gift expression. Yet Scripture repeatedly demonstrates the importance of boundaries.

Jesus limited His healing ministry to where faith was present (Matthew 13:58). Paul refused to accept payment from the Corinthian church while accepting it from others (2 Corinthians 11:7-9). Nehemiah declined meetings that would distract from his wall-building assignment (Nehemiah 6:2-3). These weren't arbitrary restrictions but strategic boundaries that preserved purpose and power.

One sister I know is a professional photographer. One day a month, she does photography solely for Kingdom work (like taking photos for a missionary family or a church event) at no charge, as her "first-fruits" to God. She testifies it keeps her love for photography alive and well, preventing burnout from client work alone.

Another minister established that she would never speak at events where she couldn't spend time privately ministering to leaders. This boundary ensures her gift remains relational, not transactional.

Ask the Lord how you can guard the sacred nature of what you carry. He will give you wisdom.

SETTING WISE LIMITATIONS

Consider these areas where boundaries might protect your gift's sacredness:

1. **Time boundaries -** Specific days or hours reserved for creative flow without interruption; sabbath rhythms that prevent burnout.

2. **Financial boundaries -** Clear guidelines about when/ where/how you receive payment for your gift versus when you freely give.

3. **Content boundaries -** Certain teachings, creations, or expressions you reserve for intimate settings rather than broad distribution.

4. **Relationship boundaries -** Discernment about which opportunities deserve your gift investment versus which ones don't align with your assignment.

5. **Platform boundaries -** Clarity about which contexts honor the nature of your gift versus which ones might compromise or dilute it.

Boundaries aren't walls, they're membranes—selectively permeable based on divine guidance rather than human pressure or financial temptation.

Jesus set the ultimate example when He withdrew from crowds demanding His healing gift to pray (Luke 5:15-16). He didn't heal everyone who wanted healing, He healed those the Father directed Him to heal (John 5:19). His boundaries weren't selfish, they were submitted—aligned with heaven's agenda rather than human demand.

GUARDING AGAINST DEPLETION

In 2 Kings 4, we find the story of Elisha and the widow's oil. When instructing her about collecting vessels for the miraculous oil, Elisha told her to borrow "empty jars—and not just a few" (v.3). The oil flowed until there were no more vessels to fill.

This principle applies to your gift—it flows as long as there are proper vessels to receive it. But without boundaries, you'll pour endlessly into improper vessels—opportunities that may seem good but aren't God, relationships that deplete rather than deploy your gift, contexts that consume your anointing without producing lasting fruit.

Guard against depletion by discerning which vessels God is asking you to fill in each season. This isn't selfishness, it's stewardship of finite human capacity carrying infinite divine potential.

SACRED EXERCISE

In which areas have you failed to establish boundaries around your gift, leading to depletion, resentment, or compromise? What divine limitations might God be asking you to honor?

SACRED PRAYER | *Master Builder, You established the boundaries of the seas and set the foundations of the Earth with divine precision. I thank You for each daughter who carries a sacred gift. Grant them supernatural wisdom to establish holy boundaries that protect what You've entrusted to them. Give them courage to maintain these boundaries even when pressure mounts to compromise. Let them discern between vessels You've called them to fill and those that would merely deplete their anointing. May they never confuse people-pleasing with servanthood or boundary-breaking with faith. Establish them* *in the freedom of divine limitations that protect their sacred purpose. In Jesus' name, Amen.*

CHAPTER 38

INTEGRATED LIFE

When your heart is in the right place, an amazing thing happens: There is *integration* between your divine calling and the practical needs of life. You won't fear monetizing what God tells you to monetize because you know it's under His direction. And you won't hesitate to turn down opportunities that don't align with your assignment, even if they promise exposure or money, because you trust God as your source.

BEYOND THE SACRED/SECULAR DIVIDE

Many of us have inherited a false divide between what's set apart and what's secular—a split often shaped more by tradition than by truth. In God's Kingdom, all ground is holy when He sends you there. This unbiblical separation has left many believers compartmentalizing their existence—being "spiritual" in certain contexts while operating by worldly wisdom in others, particularly regarding finances and career.

Scripture presents a more integrated view. Joseph administered Egypt's resources with the same spiritual wisdom he used to interpret dreams. Lydia sold purple cloth while supporting the early church. Jesus Himself was a carpenter before His public ministry began.

Your gift doesn't operate in a spiritual vacuum, separated from practical realities. Rather, it infuses those realities with Kingdom values and supernatural perspective.

DIVINE INTEGRATION IN ACTION

True integration means your ministry flows naturally from who you are, not just what you do. The businesswoman doesn't leave her prophetic gift at the boardroom door; the mother doesn't shelve her teaching anointing when helping with homework; the artist doesn't turn off her pastoral heart when creating for clients. This integration brings peace because it eliminates the exhausting compartmentalization that fragments your identity. You're not a minister on Sunday and a professional on Monday—you're a Kingdom ambassador in every context, every day.

Consider Daniel— a gifted administrator whose leadership thrived even in pagan systems. Yet beneath his public role was a prophetic mantle that revealed Heaven's secrets. The integration was seamless because his identity was secure. He wasn't "part Babylonian, part Hebrew," he was fully God's man, executing Kingdom purpose in a foreign context. I've lived this integration firsthand. I remember when one of the banks I advise asked if I would testify on their behalf in support of a historic merger between two major financial institutions. The setting? A high-security, high-stakes hearing before the Federal Reserve Bank Board and the Board of Governors for the FDIC. There were snipers on the roof, national bank CEOs in the room, and influential political leaders seated within arm's reach.

But I didn't step in as just a brand strategist or board advisor, I stepped in fully integrated as a Kingdom leader. I spoke with the authority of the Holy Spirit in a language the marketplace could understand, and more importantly, feel. By the time I finished my presentation, I could sense the presence of God so strongly that I heard some of the board members audibly clear their throats, visibly moved in a space not known for spiritual sensitivity.

Afterward, bank presidents escorted me to the door, not to thank me for representing the merger, but to thank me for representing my values so boldly and eloquently. It felt like a semi-deliverance service in a federal finance building, with executives meeting me in the lobby, extending their hands and business cards, offering support and saying, "If you ever need anything, we want to help."

This is what divine integration looks like. Not preaching a sermon—becoming one.

Living this way brings peace. You move at the rhythm of Heaven, not at the frantic pace of competition or survival. You begin to truly enjoy using your gift again, like when you first discovered it.

Proverbs 3:5–6 instructs, "Trust in the LORD with all your heart and lean not on your own understanding; in all your ways submit to Him, and He will make your paths straight." Notice it doesn't say "in your spiritual ways," but "in all your ways." Every aspect of life—financial decisions, career moves, creative projects, relationship investments—falls under this promise of divine direction.

THE HARMONY OF PROVISION
AND PURPOSE

When your gift operates from integrated identity rather than compartmentalized roles, an amazing alignment occurs between provision and purpose. You'll find yourself naturally drawn to opportunities that both meet practical needs and fulfill spiritual assignment.

Picture yourself like a musician who loves to play for the sheer beauty of the music, and trust that as you do, the Listener who matters most (God) ensures the right people hear it at the right time. You don't have to strive, you just have to be faithful.

Remember how Jesus multiplied loaves and fish to feed thousands? The miracle met practical hunger while demonstrating spiritual truth. This is divine integration—addressing tangible needs with heavenly supply. Your gift can operate with this same harmony, meeting real-world needs while revealing Kingdom reality.

The integrated life is not about perfectionism but about wholeness. It's about bringing your full self—including your gift—into every context, allowing the Spirit to determine how that gift expresses itself in each unique situation. Sometimes boldly, sometimes subtly, but always authentically.

As you allow this integration to mature, something beautiful emerges: a life without compartments, where your gift flows naturally whether in ministry settings or marketplace contexts, whether compensated or freely given, whether publicly celebrated or privately expressed. This is the abundant life Jesus promised—not fragmented, but whole.

YOUR GIFT IS A HOLY ASSIGNMENT

Oh Divine, as we conclude this chapter, let me speak with Kingdom urgency to your spirit. What Heaven has placed within you—your Signature Gift Set—is not a side project, not a hobby, not even a career path. It is a holy assignment, a sacred trust between you and the Father.

When God searched for someone to carry this particular expression of His heart to this generation, He chose you. Not because you were the most qualified by human standards, but because He saw in you a vessel He could shape for this precise purpose.

Moses initially resisted his assignment, citing inadequacy: "Who am I that I should go to Pharaoh and bring the Israelites out of Egypt?" (Exodus 3:11). God's response was profound: "I will be with you" (v.12). The qualification wasn't Moses' ability but God's presence.

Similarly, your qualification isn't your talent, education, or network. It's His presence accompanying your obedience. The assignment is holy not because you're flawless in executing it, but because the One who commissioned you is holy.

Esther faced a pivotal moment when Mordecai reminded her, "And who knows but that you have come to your royal position for such a time as this?" (Esther 4:14). Her position—like your gift—wasn't random chance but divine appointment. The assignment was bigger than her comfort, safety, or ambition.

Your gift is not about building your kingdom but advancing His. It's not about creating your legacy but fulfilling His purposes in your generation. When viewed through this lens, the temptation to commercialize, compromise, or compartmentalize your gift dissolves in the light of its eternal purpose.

Not to dwell on this – but this doesn't mean you never receive compensation or recognition. It means these outcomes never become your primary motivation. Like Jesus, who "for the joy set before him endured the cross" (Hebrews 12:2), your eyes remain fixed on the eternal impact, not the temporal reward.

Remember the parable of the talents (Matthew 25:14-30). The master didn't reward the servants based on the amount they received but on their faithful stewardship of what was entrusted. Your assignment isn't to imitate another's gift or platform; it's to faithfully steward what He's specifically placed in your hands.

Guard this perspective fiercely. The world will constantly pressure you to reduce your holy assignment to a marketable asset. Resist this reduction. Your gift deserves better. The Giver deserves better. The generation waiting for your unique expression deserves better.

You are not the world's brand, you are sacred. You are a daughter. Your gift is not a product, it's a prophecy. Your calling is not a career, it's a commission from the King of kings.

Walk in this truth, and you'll find yourself operating not from striving but from rest, not from pressure but from peace, not from comparison but from confidence in your unique design and divine assignment.

SACRED EXERCISE

How would your approach to your gift change if you consistently viewed it as a holy assignment rather than a personal possession? What specific attitudes or activities would shift?

SACRED PRAYER | *Father of Lights, from whom every good and perfect gift comes, I thank You for each Divine daughter and Sacred sister reading these words. In the authority of Jesus' name, I now commission them afresh into the consecrated stewardship of their Signature Gift Set.*

I break the power of every corrupt mindset that has reduced their holy calling to mere commodity. I shatter the chains of comparison, validation-seeking, and performance that have restricted the pure flow of their anointing. I rebuke the spirit of Mammon that has attempted to commercialize what You sanctified.

In its place, I release the spirit of wisdom and revelation in the knowledge of Christ. Let them see with perfect clarity the holy purpose behind their unique design. Let them hear with supernatural precision the specific assignment You've entrusted to them in this hour.

I declare over them, "You are not for sale! Your gift is not merchandise! Your calling is not a career path! You are a chosen vessel, a royal priesthood, a daughter of destiny carrying a holy assignment that will echo into eternity."

I commission you to operate not by the world's wisdom but by the Spirit's leading. I release you from the pressure to produce and propel you into the freedom to flow. I remove the heavy yoke of human expectation and place upon you the easy yoke of divine partnership.

May your gift once again fill you with wonder rather than burden you with weight. May you reclaim the joy of your first love as you minister not to gain approval but to give glory. May you walk in such perfect integration of identity and assignment that your very presence shifts atmospheres without striving.

Rise up, daughter of Zion! Take your place in the divine narrative! Steward your holy assignment with courage, clarity, and conviction, knowing that the One who called you is faithful, and He will do it.

For His glory alone, Amen.

The Pace of Grace

TRADING HUSTLE FOR HEAVEN'S RHYTHM

CHAPTER 39

SURRENDERED STRENGTH

"Come with me by yourselves to a quiet place and get some rest." –
Mark 6:31 (NIV)

I know—it seems I'm not ready to put rest to bed just yet. Heaven keeps bringing us back here for a reason. In this chapter, we're not just talking about rest; we're going to live it. Together, we'll peel back the layers of hustle, hurry, and high-functioning fatigue that too many of us have mistaken for faithfulness.

We live in a world that glorifies the grind—early mornings, late nights, and constant doing in the name of "purpose." But Heaven doesn't run on hustle. The Kingdom has its own cadence. It moves in the pace of grace.

In God's economy, rest is not a luxury or reward for finishing your to-do list, it's a requirement for living well. This chapter is your invitation to unlearn frantic productivity and step into the unforced rhythms of grace (Matthew 11:28–30, The Message).

You've heard me mention before that the irony is, when you align with Heaven's timing, you actually accomplish more, not less. Grace accomplishes in a moment what human effort takes years to achieve. Let's explore how to synchronize our lives with Heaven's rhythm—a pace where your soul can breathe, your heart can listen, and your work can flourish without overwhelming your peace.

STRIVING VS. ABIDING: THE CALL TO HOLY REST

From the very beginning, God modeled a rhythm of rest, not due to exhaustion, but to establish a divine blueprint. So why, then, do we treat rest like a reward to be earned instead of a rhythm to be honored? Why do we hesitate to receive what Heaven freely modeled? How often do we find ourselves pushing beyond the grace, treating rest as optional or wasteful? Honestly, maybe I'm preaching this part so passionately because I need the reminder too. Sometimes the teacher has to teach herself—again and again—until it finally takes root. The call to holy rest is not merely about taking a day off, it's about entering a state of trust. Hebrews 4:10 says, "For anyone who enters God's rest also rests from their works, just as God did from His" (NKJV). This is an invitation to cease endless self-effort and live in surrendered reliance.

When the Israelites were delivered from slavery in Egypt, they had to learn how to live as free people. Slaves can't rest; sons and daughters can. In the wilderness, God reintroduced the Sabbath, a radical concept for formerly oppressed people. It was a sign of trust. Would they believe manna would fall again tomorrow if they didn't gather on the seventh day? Some didn't. They went out to work on the day of rest and found nothing (Exodus 16:27). God was teaching them, "I will provide for you; you don't have to toil incessantly."

So it is with you. You're not in Egypt anymore. Stop living like you're enslaved to the grind. You are a child of God on Kingdom assignment. And your Father can do more with six surrendered days—or even twenty-three yielded hours—than you could ever accomplish in seven anxious, self-striving ones. Jesus extends this invitation plainly in the Gospels. When the disciples were exhausted from ministry, He didn't say "work harder." He said, "Come with me by yourselves to a quiet place and get some rest" (Mark 6:31). Rest is not retreat when it's spent with Jesus, it's refueling.

Dalton-Smith's research confirms what Scripture has shown all along: burnout often comes not from doing too much, but from not receiving enough of God's replenishment. When we embrace rest as holy, we recover not just our energy, but our joy and clarity.

Think about it: if the enemy can't tempt you with outright sin, he'd love to wear you out with overwork. A burned-out believer is just as sidelined as a morally fallen one. Satan loses much of his foothold when we choose rest, because rest says, "I trust God, not myself." When you rest, you declare that God is on the throne, holding all things together while you step aside. That is an act of worship.

Christian therapist and author Dr. Anita Phillips insightfully notes that when we refuse to rest, we're not just tired, we're actually refusing to trust God's care. It's like telling Him, "I got this; I don't need Your Sabbath gift." How it must grieve His heart when we live like orphans struggling to survive instead of children leaning on His provision.

So right here, reject the lie that rest equals laziness. Embrace the truth that rest (when led by the Spirit) equals faith. It's a holy rhythm: work *from* rest, not rest *from* work. Adam's first day alive was God's day of rest. Man's first full day was enjoyed in God's finished work. We start from rest. We start by receiving.

BREAKING THE HUSTLE CULTURE

He said, "Take my yoke upon you ... My yoke is easy and my burden is light" (Matthew 11:29-30). If what you're carrying feels harsh and heavy, it's not His yoke. That doesn't mean there's no burden or work, but it will feel "light" and "easy" with Him. Like two oxen plowing together, He takes the brunt, you're just walking in step with the Strong One.

If you've been feeling a heavy, joyless weight, pause and check: Did I pick up something God didn't assign? Am I dragging a load alone that I should be sharing with Holy Spirit? Often the answer is yes, and the solution is simple: repent (change your mind) and realign.

God may prompt you to prune some activities or re-prioritize time with family or Him. Trust His lead. When you create margin, you make space for God to move.

THE GIFT OF SLEEP AND SELAH

It seems almost too basic to mention, but one of the most spiritual things you can do is get enough sleep. The psalmist says God "grants sleep to those He loves" (Psalm 127:2). Instead of burning midnight oil every night, perhaps the holier choice is to turn off the computer, say "Selah" (pause), and go to bed. Your body and mind are temples of the Holy Spirit; they need renewal.

Do I constantly need this reminder and holy conviction? Absolutely. I'm naturally a night person. I used to say only somewhat jokingly to my news team at 3:00 a.m. before my morning show, *"I don't feel the anointing until about ten or eleven—and even then, with coffee."* Similarly, King David, a man of war and worship, wrote, "He makes me lie down in green pastures, He leads me beside quiet waters, He refreshes my soul" (Psalm 23:2–3). Sometimes God has to make us lie down because otherwise we wouldn't. But it's there that He refreshes us.

Bottom line: If kings like David, spiritual giants, needed physical rest and spiritual renewal, so do we. Denying that is pride or ignorance. Embracing it is wisdom and humility.

RESTORING YOUR RHYTHMS

Modern life has thrown many of us out of sync with Heaven's rhythm (hello, 24/7 connectivity). We weren't designed to run on constant input and output. That's why we have to be intentional about restoring patterns of Sabbath and Selah not just in our weeks, but in the ordinary rhythm of our days.

Trust me, I'm not just teaching this platinum lesson—I'm a student too. As a recovering perfectionist married to the Energizer bunny, I often have to remind myself to slow down, to breathe, and to come back to rest. I'm in remission from grind—and sometimes I relapse.

So, if you feel like you're learning this in real time? You're not alone. I'm right here with you.

What might this look like practically?

- **Daily:** Find small "selah" moments. Maybe a ten-minute break to step outside and breathe, thank God, reset your mind. Perhaps a cut-off time in the evening for work so you can wind down with the Lord or your loved ones.

- **Weekly:** Honor a Sabbath principle. Choose a day (or a portion of a day, if a whole day feels impossible) where you do things that rejuvenate you and connect you to God. This might be Sunday, or another day depending on your life. Protect it. Let emails wait, let chores sit undone for a bit. The world won't fall apart. In fact, you'll find the world looks brighter afterward.

- **Seasonally:** Recognize your limits in different seasons. There are busy harvest times, and there should be winter times of more rest. If you've just come through an intense period (a big project, a new baby, a family crisis), it's okay and necessary to recuperate. Do not expect constant output from yourself. Even the strongest soil needs time to rest if it's going to keep producing good fruit.

- **Spiritually:** Incorporate times of personal retreat. Maybe once or twice a year, take a day or weekend if you can to unplug with God, worship, and dream without the to-do list. These can be times of enormous refilling and recalibration.

And while you're setting aside time with Him, remember this: don't rest from God—rest with God. He's not just in church and prayer meetings. He can be in the quiet cup of tea on your porch, in the laughter during a family game, in the pages of a good book that feeds your soul (ahem ... clears throat ... possibly this book?). Father God also leads you beside still waters, not just to intercede there but to enjoy His presence there.

THE PRODUCTIVITY PARADOX

Remember the productivity paradox we discussed earlier—the Kingdom's rhythm where rest multiplies results. Here's a delightful secret: when you operate at Heaven's pace, you often get more done in less time. It's like how tithing (giving 10%) causes the 90% to go further than 100% ever could without God's blessing. Similarly, resting—tithing your time in trust—causes your working hours to be far more Spirit-empowered.

Suddenly, inspired ideas drop in those same days of trial and error. Divine connections align that move things forward faster than months of striving ever could. God is still the God of "suddenly." In Scripture, when people aligned with His rhythm, miraculous acceleration often followed their obedient stillness.

It's a paradox. By not always working, you actually invite God to work more powerfully on your behalf. As Isaiah 30:15 reminds us, "In repentance and rest is your salvation, in quietness and trust is your strength." Rest becomes a weapon—your quiet confidence tells the enemy, "I trust God more than I trust my hustle."

Let that sink in as you sip your tea. I'm not just preaching this, I've lived it. In fact, I'm pretty sure some folks (maybe even my own husband) wanted to put me in a straitjacket when I started pulling away from the 24/7 grind. The culture makes rest look lazy or impossible. But a few years ago, my sister-in-love and I gave ourselves permission to pause. She bought us matching sweatshirts that said we were "allergic to mornings," and we wore them proudly while soaking in a little space to simply *be*—no deadlines, no demands. Just rest. And it was holy.

The world might call you irresponsible for stepping back. But results will speak. There will be a noticeable grace on your life that outpaces those who burn the candle at both ends. Even others will notice. Coworkers might say, "You always seem so calm, yet you meet your deadlines. How?" That's your opening to testify about the Prince of Peace!

TRUSTING GOD'S TIMING

Often, our refusal to rest is ultimately a refusal to trust God's timing. We fear if we slow down, we'll miss out. But consider this: If God has called you to it, He will get you there on schedule as you obey Him, which includes obeying His command to rest.

Delays can actually be divine. Maybe He withholds a platform until your character is ready (as we saw in earlier chapters). Part of character is learning patience and trust.

When it's time for you to run, you will run, and you'll do it with supernatural strength like Elijah outrunning Ahab's chariot (1 Kings 18:46) after a moment of divine empowerment. But until the Spirit says "Go," you keep step with His pace.

EMBRACE THE GRACE

"Grace" is such a beautiful word. It implies gift, ease, undeserved favor. Picture grace as a current in a river. When you move in grace, you flow *with* the current, not against it. It may still be work (paddling, steering), but the river carries you. When you strive in flesh, you're fighting upstream, which is exhausting and ultimately futile.

So ask daily, "God, where's Your grace flowing today? Let me follow that." Sometimes the grace is on tackling a big task (and wow, you blitz through it). Other times, grace beckons you to close the laptop and play with your kids or call your mom back (and later that evening, a solution to a problem pops into your mind unsolicited. Grace gave it while you rested).

Grace also manifests as peace. "Let the peace of Christ rule in your hearts" (Colossians 3:15). In the original Greek the word "rule" literally means to act like an umpire—to decide what's safe, what's off, and what's aligned. So if you're losing peace about how you're living or working, pay attention. Peace might be signaling you to slow down, adjust, or shift course.

To live at the pace of grace, you must become attuned to those internal Holy Spirit signals. He will prompt you: "Enough for today, daughter." He might remind you that He loves you not for your productivity but because you're His. Sometimes He'll orchestrate a circumstance to force rest. Ever gotten sick right after overdoing it? I'm not saying sickness is from God, but He can use even that to make you lie down and reevaluate.

Better to choose rest by wisdom than be forced into it by collapse.

Let's flip the script on hustle. As a Kingdom woman, you don't "rise and grind," you rise and abide. You don't "chase paper," you chase His presence. Ironically, goodness and mercy chase you (Psalm 23:6) when you dwell in the Shepherd's house. The blessings overtake the obedient (Deuteronomy 28:2).

My sister, exhale. Loosen your clenched fingers a bit from the steering wheel of life. The scenery of destiny will not pass you by. In fact, with more open eyes (not blurry from fatigue), you'll catch Heaven's breadcrumbs more easily.

A NEW RHYTHM

Imagine waking up rested, spending unrushed time with God, and then tackling your day with focus and calm. Imagine punctuating your work with moments of prayer or a short walk, hearing birds or feeling the sun, reminding you that the world is bigger than what's on your screen. Imagine ending the day with gratitude and without anxiety gnawing at your gut. It may seem easier said than done, but try the Holy Spirit. Ask for your sacred schedule in this season. This doesn't have to be a dream; it is possible when you adopt Heaven's rhythm.

But it takes intentionality and faith. Faith that God can multiply time, that He can keep you on track even if you take a break, that He values you over what you produce.

It's countercultural, yes. Some won't understand when you say, "I don't do meetings on Sundays," or "I turn my phone off after eight," or "I can't take on that extra project right now." But the fruit will prove wisdom's children right (Luke 7:35). You will be healthier, happier, holier, a better leader, a kinder mother, a more creative entrepreneur, because you honor how God designed you.

So break agreement with hustle and hurry. They are not your masters. Jesus is. And His pace leads to green pastures.

Embrace the pace of grace. It's slower, yes. But like a well-tuned melody, it's beautifully slower. And when you dance to that tempo, you'll find Heaven syncs perfectly with your steps.

SACRED EXERCISE

Where are you afraid to slow down, and why? Is there a fear that if you rest, things will fall apart or you'll lose out? Speak God's truth into that fear For example, "God upholds all things, including my work, by His word" or "He gives to His beloved even in their sleep" (Psalm 127:2).

Remember: a hurried woman can miss divine moments, but a paced woman hears God's whispers. The world needs what you carry, yes, but it needs the grace-infused you, not the drained you. In rest, you are refilled. In trust, you become unshakable. And in that state, you truly become a bearer of God's glory, not just in what you do, but in who you are.

CHAPTER 40

FROM ENSLAVED TO ENTHRONED

The journey from hustle to holy rhythm is, at its core, a journey from slavery to daughtership, from toiling to trusting, from striving to reigning. It reflects the fundamental shift in identity Christ purchased for us. No longer do we live as orphans scrambling to secure our place, but as daughters seated with Christ in heavenly places (Ephesians 2:6).

When you embrace Kingdom rhythms, you're not just practicing better self-care or seeking work-life balance. You're making a prophetic declaration about who God is and who you are in Him. You're declaring that He is a good Father, not a taskmaster. That you are a beloved daughter, not a hired servant. That grace, not grind, is the engine of the Kingdom. That rest is not weakness, but reverence. This is spiritual warfare at its most subtle and powerful. Every time you choose rest over striving, every time you honor Sabbath over hustle, every time you move at Heaven's pace rather than the world's pressure—you're dismantling the enemy's age-old lie that your worth comes from your work.

This is an exodus of the heart—stepping out of Egypt's rhythm and into the cadence of the Kingdom. The taskmaster's whip is not your drumbeat. In Christ, you are released from relentless proving and invited into unforced rhythms of grace: producing exceptional fruit without exceptional wear, carrying peace amid pressure, moving with supernatural effectiveness while honoring sacred rest.

Remember Eve's temptation? At its root was the suggestion that God was withholding something good, that she needed to grasp for herself what wasn't being freely given. This same lie drives much of our frenetic activity today—the fear that if we don't strive endlessly, we'll miss out on what others have.

But you, Divine, know better. You've tasted the freedom of moving with His current rather than against it. You've felt joy return where performance once stole wonder. You've sensed Him realigning your steps to His timing, rekindling childlike faith that sits at His feet before running in His name. You've glimpsed what it means to accomplish more by doing less—because the less is empowered by His more. This is what it looks like to be established as a woman of both authority and rest—knowing when to advance and when to be still, when to speak and when to listen.

SACRED EXERCISE

In what ways have you been measuring your worth by your productivity? How has this affected your relationship with God, your sense of identity, and your physical and emotional well-being? What specific lies about achievement, success, and worth do you need to renounce? What truths from this chapter do you need to embrace?

SACRED PRAYER | *In Jesus' name, I release you from the taskmaster's rhythm and bless you with the cadence of the Kingdom. May joy be restored where grind stole wonder; may your steps be realigned to God's perfect timing. Be established as a woman of authority and rest—bearing exceptional fruit from a place of worship, not wear. Let delay become divine, waiting become worship, and rest become revolutionary. I seal this alignment over your life in the mighty name of Jesus. Amen.*

Now, having established a foundation of identity, gifting, purity of motive, and restful rhythm, you are ready to build legacy. In the next chapter, we'll shift our gaze from our personal journey to the impact God wants to have through us for generations. Get ready to think long-term and big-picture, without losing the sacred center we've cultivated thus far.

Let There
Be Legacy

CHAPTER 41

GENERATIONAL EYES

It flows directly from your Sacred Identity journey into themes of impact, inheritance, social justice, and long-term influence. In this chapter, we shift our gaze from personal breakthrough to generational purpose. What does it mean to build something that outlives you, to sow seeds that others will reap? God's heart is not just for you and your lifetime. He is the God of Abraham, Isaac, and Jacob, thinking three generations at a time (Exodus 3:15). He's inviting you to join Him in legacy building.

Legacy isn't about ego, it's about eternal effect. It's the difference between temporary excitement and true, sustained transformation that multiplies beyond your direct reach. This chapter will challenge and equip you to heal any hindrances to legacy (like wounds that limit your voice) so you can set your sights on influence that is both holy and far-reaching.

On that note, Pastor Mike Connell—who ministers powerfully in inner healing and deliverance—often teaches that unhealed wounds can sabotage our calling if left unaddressed. Think of it: A leader might build an impressive ministry, but if she carries unresolved rejection, she may unconsciously push people away or burn out seeking validation. A mother might try to impart faith to her kids, but if she's shackled by fear from past trauma, that fear can transfer despite her best intentions. We must let God heal us deeply if we want our influence to be deep and lasting. As a wise builder strengthens a foundation before adding stories to a house, so God strengthens your soul through inner healing and spiritual freedom. Embrace His healing work now through prayer, counsel, and forgiveness so that cracks are sealed and the enemy has no foothold. With a whole heart, you'll be able to carry a whole legacy, unmarred by hidden fractures.

We'll explore how to navigate warfare over your voice, the necessity of inner healing as a builder, and why your work and voice matter for such a time as this. Get ready: God is moving you from thinking only of your life to thinking of your lineage and impact.

CHAPTER 42

GIFTS DON'T DIE WITH YOU

There are some things God entrusts to you that were never meant to expire when your body does.

Spiritual gifts, when discerned, developed, and deployed, are more than momentary graces. They are legacy tools meant to bless generations. Gifts don't die with you, they can multiply beyond you.

God is not looking for one-generation wonders. He never has been. From Abraham to David to Jesus, God works in lineage. He plants an oak that will give shade to many after you. It's time to lift your eyes from mere survival or success and start thinking about succession: Who and what will carry on the work when you're gone?

Legacy, in the Kingdom, is not something we wait until retirement to think about. It's not something reserved for the elderly or famous. If you have influence in any capacity (and you do), you can start investing in legacy now. This means two practical things: mentoring and modeling. Mentoring those coming behind, and modeling a faithfulness that can be replicated.

Many women have been taught to view their spiritual gifts as personal assignments, something between them and God only. But Scripture and history show the most impactful lives intentionally pass the baton.

Consider David. He had the heart to build God a temple, but that assignment went to Solomon. Yet David wasn't prideful or passive; he gathered materials, drew up plans, and charged Solomon to finish the work. David's legacy wasn't in four walls he built, but in the son he equipped and the worship culture he established for Israel.

Similarly, Esther's legacy wasn't just her saving the Jews in her lifetime, it was the festival of Purim that continues to this day, and the inspiration she gives to every believer to stand in the gap. She mentored through modeling courage and intercession.

I may not have children in the natural, but I am a spiritual mother and sacred midwife to hundreds of young and seasoned women. I often ask myself, "What would happen if I didn't think generationally? What if I didn't put in the time, prayer, and serious effort to document the truths and revelation you're now reading in this book?" Imagine not having language for your Sacred Identity. How selfish it would be to let divine intel from Heaven go with me to the grave.

Now put yourself in that same space. What are you carrying that was never meant to end with you? Let there be legacy beyond our days and lifetime. Let there be fruit that lives on after your voice has gone silent. This is how we die empty and live full.

The Proverbs 31 woman also models legacy: "Her children rise up and call her blessed" and "give her the reward she has earned"

(Prov 31:28, 31). She built a life that benefited her household and community long-term.

These biblical figures didn't see their gifts as isolated or just for self-fulfillment. They saw them as a trust for the next generation.

Now, so must we.

Dr. Myles Munroe heartbreakingly illustrated the importance of this when he said the graveyard is the richest place on Earth—rich with books never written, songs never sung, and dreams never realized. He urged believers not to take their God-given treasure to the grave. Die empty. Pour it out while you live, so when you leave this Earth, you leave it brighter, wiser, holier. In other words, live in such a way that the next generation is handed a torch, not left fumbling in the dark. God intends for you to deposit what He's given you into others. If you hold back out of fear or selfishness, you effectively bury those talents. But if you invest in people, you create dividends for decades to come. The richest inheritance you can leave is a life poured out for Jesus that in turn pours into others.

The sobering truth is if you don't steward your gifts with legacy in mind, something God intended to be passed on may end with you. Now let that sink in deep right there. This is especially urgent for us as Black women, our fellow sisters of color, and women as a whole in communities where representation and trailblazing are vital. Your ceiling can become someone else's floor if you build it high enough.

So what does that look like in practice? It might mean writing the book, even if you think only a few will read it, so the message is preserved. It could mean deliberately training someone younger in your skills, even if it takes extra time. It might mean recording your prayers or teachings for posterity. It certainly means living in such a way that those who observe you up close can inherit a way of life worth carrying on.

Ask the Lord: "How can my gift make room for others to flourish, even after I'm gone or I've moved to a new assignment?"

Legacy begins with that question.

CHAPTER 43

FROM ANOINTING TO ASSIGNMENT

Anointing is not the finish line, it's the starting gate.

It is entirely possible to be gifted, chosen, and affirmed, and still not be fully walking in the assignment God intends that gift to accomplish. We can enjoy the anointing and the personal spiritual high it brings, but God eventually points and says, "Now, over there, pour out into this assignment."

Here's the pivot: Up to now, much of this journey has been about you (getting whole, knowing identity, finding rhythm). Now God is saying, "It's assignment time." Not that you weren't doing anything before, but there's a fresh commissioning upon you. Anointing (the empowerment) is there—now comes the precise aim. Like an arrow drawn back and ready, God is about to release you into something targeted.

This can be scary. Maybe you think, "Lord, I'm good with the anointing in my prayer closet or local circle, but now You want me to step into *that*?" Perhaps it's a public role, a bold project, confronting an injustice, or starting a social enterprise—something that moves you beyond comfort.

Yet this is what you were prepared for. All the healing, learning, waiting, it was training camp for assignment. Heaven doesn't anoint you just so you can feel goosebumps; Heaven anoints you so you can change something on earth.

Ephesians 2:10 again: you have good works prepared in advance to walk in.

So, will you say yes to the assignment?

Mary said yes and carried the Messiah. Esther said yes and saved a nation. Each had an anointing (favor, grace) but also an assignment requiring courage. You have your own version.

Take a moment to discern if there is an inkling or open door already in front of you that you've been hesitant to embrace. Often, as we discuss assignment, *that thing* comes to mind. Maybe you've been saying, "I'm not ready," but God says, "I am, and I will be with you."

Let's bridge the gap between anointing and assignment in practical ways:

- **Identify where your gifts meet a need in the world or the Church.** That intersection often reveals an assignment. For example, your gift of teaching and passion for young people might point to writing a curriculum for youth or mentoring teen girls. Your gift of hospitality and service along with your concern for justice might converge in starting a community dinner that builds bridges across cultural divides. (If you need further gifts clarity, please refer back to the Sacred ID product offering on page 133.)

- **Accept that assignment usually looks like servanthood.** It might not be glamorous; it might even feel like a demotion before promotion (think Joseph managing a prison before managing a nation). But it will carry eternal weight. Don't be surprised if God asks you to do something "smaller" or more behind-the-scenes than you imagined; oftentimes that is the proving ground that leads to greater influence later.

- **Understand assignment can be seasonal.** Completing one doesn't mean you're done; God may have multiple missions across your life. Focus on the current assignment and do it well, trusting He'll reveal the next. David's first assignment was shepherding, later it was slaying a giant, then it was leading a nation. Same anointing (leadership, worship, courage) applied in different ways over time.

- **Recognize that assignment attracts opposition.** A clear calling often triggers clear warfare (Nehemiah built the wall and enemies showed up immediately). Don't misread resistance as a closed door—often it's confirmation you're on the right track. The key is to press through with prayer and perseverance.

If you're still unsure of your assignment, look at what's already in your hand (like God asked Moses). The seed of it is probably already present—a passion, a position you find yourself in, a problem that only you seem to notice and feel burden for. Also, remember what we discussed earlier: Get quiet with God. Sometimes the assignment is whispered, not shouted.

Anointing got you ready; assignment gets you moving.

Let's continue building, now with outward focus, carrying forward what God has done inwardly.

CHAPTER 44

THE SOCIAL IMPACT OF SACRED PEOPLE

There is a quiet but undeniable shift happening: Divine daughters are stepping up with solutions for society's deepest pains. We are in a time when social impact and sacred identity are converging. No longer is "ministry" confined to church settings—God is deploying His women into education, government, arts, business, science, justice movements, and more. Why? Because He cares about the whole world, and we carry His Kingdom into these spheres.

This is part of your assignment too. Sacred identity is deeply personal, but it's never meant to be private. We are called to be change agents. Jesus said we are salt and light (Matthew 5:13–16), transformative agents in the world. Light doesn't fight darkness by yelling at it; it simply shines and darkness flees. Salt doesn't need to protest blandness; it just is present, and flavor and preservation happen. By being fully who God made you and boldly where God sends you, you change atmospheres.

Think of historical examples: The Hebrew midwives Shiphrah and Puah quietly defied Pharaoh's decree and saved countless infant lives—a courageous social impact (Exodus 1:17–21). Deborah, a judge, led Israel in battle and governance, securing peace for forty years—national impact (Judges 4–5). In more recent history, Christian women like Sojourner Truth and Harriet Tubman, fueled by faith, fought slavery and freed many. They lived out sacred identity in social action.

Harriet Tubman in particular testified that it was the voice of God guiding her northward that enabled her success. She would stop to pray and wait for divine guidance during her rescue missions. That partnership with God made her efforts incredibly effective; she never lost a single passenger on the Underground Railroad. Harriet's legacy shows spiritual obedience has social consequences. By following God's whispers, she changed hundreds of lives and inspired millions more. The faith that sustained her in secret empowered her public bravery.

Perhaps God has burdened your heart with a social issue like human trafficking, youth mentorship, racial reconciliation, or community development. That burden is likely an invitation to do something about it. As you'll recall from earlier chapters, Sacred Identity helps you discern who you are and what Heaven placed within you. From there, your mantle begins to take public form—a transition we'll unpack later as identity matures into influence. And when that inner calling takes outward shape, it naturally draws you toward issues that matter to God's heart—justice, compassion, and restoration.

We must move beyond vague encouragement into prophetic clarity in these areas. It's not enough to say "God cares about justice." We must let Him use us to *do* justice. Sacred people can bring sacred solutions. Maybe it's starting a social enterprise/nonprofit, or advocating for policy change, or bringing a prayer group into city hall, or mentoring at-risk youth, or creating jobs in underserved areas.

It's time to dream bigger about the social impact of your calling. Your ministry may be nurtured within the church, but its reach is meant to extend far beyond the walls. God is sending you into culture, not away from it. The same anointing that makes you a powerful intercessor can make you a brilliant entrepreneur who funds Kingdom projects. Speaking of funds, women called to be mentored and midwifed by me will build and birth entities that bring forth both Kingdom impact and income at the same time. In fact, that same prophetic insight you use in prayer can become strategy downloads for community reform. God has no secular/sacred divide. All ground is His ground, and He's giving you every place you step (Joshua 1:3) for His glory.

To do this effectively, consider the wisdom of strategic planning. Even in secular fields, those who bring change work intentionally. In the business world, innovators like Larry Keeley of Doblin Group emphasize that lasting change comes through thoughtful, multifaceted strategy. They don't rely on one flashy idea; they integrate many elements (networks, processes, user experience) to make an innovation stick. This wisdom isn't foreign to us, it originates from God, the ultimate strategist. So as you pursue your assignment, pray and plan. Ask God for both inspired ideas *and* practical steps. He may lead you to research, to partner with others, or to acquire new skills, all as part of expanding your influence. This doesn't mean relying on the flesh; it means stewarding the vision with sanctified intelligence. Imagine Nehemiah rebuilding Jerusalem's walls. He prayed for favor *and* he carefully surveyed the ruins at night, organized workers by families, and set up guards (Nehemiah 4). Spiritual work and practical strategy, hand in hand. You are capable of the same dual approach.

We should never shy away from learning best practices or seeking professional knowledge in our area of calling. If God calls you to education reform, study effective educational models; if to business, learn from proven ethical business leaders. God can use this knowledge, breathed on by His Spirit, to give you exceptional favor and results. The world will see the combination of God's presence *and* godly excellence in and through you.

At the same time, remain dependent on God throughout. We plan our way, but He directs our steps (Proverbs 16:9). Be flexible when He interrupts your plan with a Holy Spirit surprise. It's a dance: we prepare the horse for battle, but victory comes from the Lord (Proverbs 21:31).

We must also prepare for spiritual resistance. When you step into arenas long held by darkness, expect pushback. It might be human opposition or unseen warfare. But take heart, because "Greater is He that is in you than he that is in the world" (1 John 4:4). We'll delve into warfare in the next chapter. The main point here is your influence in society is part of God's rescue mission for people. The enemy won't like it, but he is powerless against a daughter of the King walking in obedience and covered in prayer.

Legacy is not just about personal succession; it's about Kingdom advancement. It's about laying groundwork now that will answer someone's prayers fifty years from now.

Think of those who fought for women's right to vote, or to preach, or for racial equality, and how we benefit from their legacy. Likewise, what you pioneer now will enable those after you to run further. Perhaps your ceiling will indeed be their floor—and wouldn't that make our Pappa smile?

CHAPTER 45

WARFARE OVER YOUR VOICE

The moment you decide to be a voice in this world and not just an echo, warfare intensifies. The enemy has always feared the voices of God's Divine—from Eve (whom Satan targeted first) to Deborah to the women who discovered Jesus' empty tomb and carried the first resurrection announcement. A woman's voice carrying God's Word is a force hell cannot withstand, so hell fights tooth and nail to silence or disqualify that voice.

If he's attacking your confidence, it's because your bold voice terrifies him. If he's attacking relationships, it's because unity in your team or family will stomp on his plans. If he's attacking your health, it's perhaps to sap your energy so you'll quit your assignment. So flip the script. See every attack as a backhanded compliment that you're on the right track. The areas of greatest warfare often highlight the areas of greatest calling.

Stand firm then, with the belt of truth, breastplate of righteousness, shoes of peace, shield of faith, helmet of salvation, and sword of the Spirit (Eph 6:14–17). You are fully armed. And remember to rest in warfare too—the battle is the Lord's. He's the Commander of Angel Armies and He has your back. Often, simply standing and refusing to quit is the victory.

So if you've encountered unusual conflict or obstacles since stepping out, don't be discouraged. You're not doing something wrong, you're likely doing something very right. Surround yourself with prayer warriors. Cover your endeavor in intercession. Do not battle alone, recruit others to pray with and for you. Moses needed Aaron and Hur to hold up his arms on the hill so the battle in the valley could be won (Exodus 17:12). Identify your Aaron and Hur—those who will lift you in prayer when you grow weary.

Also, guard against offense and division. The enemy loves to divide teams and allies through misunderstandings. Keep short accounts, forgive quickly, and communicate openly, because often the real enemy is not the person irritating you, it's the devil trying to derail the mission. Link shields with your sacred sisters and press on together.

SACRED EXERCISE

Where do you need to reclaim your voice or authority after yielding to intimidation? Visualize taking it back with Jesus' help and declare it. For example: "I reclaim my voice in my workplace that I silenced out of fear. I will speak the truth in love boldly."

Remember, the warfare isn't about you personally – it's about the threat you pose to darkness. If you were insignificant, the enemy would ignore you. But you are a key player in God's Kingdom agenda, so you're a target. This realization shouldn't scare you; it should embolden you. Hell has taken notice of you, which means Heaven's purpose in you is major. You fight *from* victory, not for victory. Jesus already disarmed principalities at the cross (Colossians 2:15). We enforce the victory through prayer, truth, and courage, but the outcome is secure in Christ.

CHAPTER 46

LEAVE SOME FOR THE FIELD

Divine, the time has come to carry your gift beyond the familiar walls. As you recall, in ancient Israel, harvesters were commanded to leave some grain at the edges of their fields so the poor and strangers could glean and be fed (Leviticus 19:9–10). In the same way, not everything God gives you is meant to be kept within the four walls of the church or your inner circle. There are people in the "fields" of the world who are waiting to taste and see what He's deposited in you. Leave some for the field.

Perhaps you've poured your anointing only into church services or private circles, but Heaven is urging you outward. That might mean sharing your story in a public forum, launching a community initiative, or bringing faith-informed solutions into your industry. This isn't casting pearls to swine, it's casting bread upon the waters (Ecclesiastes 11:1) in faith that it will nourish whoever God sends your way.

Your sacred assignment isn't meant to hide in safe spaces. It's meant to transform spaces. The same God who met you at the altar now calls you into the marketplace. He's expanding your influence so His love and power can reach the hearts of those who would never step into a sanctuary. You carry the Kingdom within you, and the fields of society are ripe for harvest (John 4:35). It's time to go where He leads, even if it's outside your comfort zone.

As you step out, remember that legacy isn't built by staying where it's comfortable. Legacy is built when a daughter of God dares to shine His light in dark places. Heaven goes with you into those boardrooms, classrooms, slums, and stages. The same Spirit that moved in your prayer closet will move in the public square. Trust Him. Leave the safety nets behind and watch God show up mightily in the field of your calling.

As we head into the final section, know this: You are being positioned for influence not for your sake, but for His name and the sake of those connected to your obedience. We'll talk about being crowned for influence and stepping fully into sacred visibility and impact with wisdom and worship.

SACRED EXERCISE

What part of your gifting or message is God asking you to take "into the field"? Who outside your usual sphere might God be aiming to bless through you? Write down any names or groups that come to heart and pray over them.

Where have you perhaps held back (out of fear or habit) from engaging with the broader world? What would "leaving grain in the field" look like practically for you this coming season?

Generations wait for what you carry. Nations, even, will be impacted by the ripple effect of your faithful obedience beyond the church's four walls.

So Divine, leave some for the field. Sow generously. Our God is Lord of the harvest, and He won't let a single seed of yours fall to the ground in vain.

As you step boldly into the field, don't miss this crucial truth: what you build externally must be sustained internally. You can sow widely, but if you're leaking from within, your impact will eventually stall. This is where internal freedom becomes the true fuel of lasting legacy.

CHAPTER 47

BUILD BIG, BUT STAY FREE: WHY HEALING STILL MATTERS

Dr. Caroline Leaf, a cognitive neuroscientist and author, has spent decades studying the science of thought. Her pioneering research on neuroplasticity confirms what Scripture has long revealed: The way we think shapes the way we live. She demonstrates how toxic thought patterns create restrictive neural pathways, while renewed, Scripture-aligned thinking (Romans 12:2) literally rewires the brain for clarity, healing, and expanded capacity. Your freedom journey physically restructures your brain for expanded influence. When your mind aligns with God's truth, your brain follows, activating the blueprint of your Kingdom influence.

Freedom isn't a finish line—it's a framework. From that framework flow three guiding truths every anointed builder must carry: freedom determines capacity, healing prepares expansion, and sustaining that freedom is your sacred responsibility—it's not a single breakthrough, but a way of life.

Your ministry's current ceiling directly correlates to your present freedom level. This isn't limiting but clarifying—you build according to your healing, not beyond it. As Jesus taught, "Everyone who is fully trained will be like their teacher" (Luke 6:40). You reproduce your actual freedom, not your theoretical understanding of freedom. That's why some ministries plateau despite sound teaching—the leader's unaddressed bondage creates an invisible ceiling. The good news? As your inner healing deepens, external impact naturally expands without striving. Freedom fuels fruitfulness—no striving required.

Healing, too, is not just personal, it's Kingdom preparation. The freedom work you prioritize today directly prepares tomorrow's influence expansion. This reframes healing from self-improvement to Kingdom investment. Every therapy session, prayer ministry appointment, or forgiveness process becomes strategic preparation for increased impact. Moses experienced this pattern. His anger healing in Midian directly enabled his leadership effectiveness when facing Pharaoh. Similarly, your current healing focus likely addresses the exact area that would otherwise limit your next assignment. The wound you're healing now is often the wall between you and your next level.

MY HEALING IN REAL TIME

I know what it's like to look healed on the outside but still carry residue on the inside. During one of my regular SEO Days (monthly consecrated time with my Sovereign Executive Officer), the Lord led me into a soul-level purge. As a visual learner, I grabbed color-coded sticky notes and created columns, naming people and situations where I felt deep offense. But Daddy didn't stop there. Soon the list included those I harbored resentment, envy, and even bitterness toward. As I looked at that wall of pain, I realized that if some of these deep-seated emotions had been left unchecked, a few could have tiptoed toward hate.

It was hard to confront, but if I couldn't be honest, naked, and unfiltered before my King, who was I really fooling? That day marked a turning point. I saw clearly how unchecked emotions could silently sabotage what I was called to steward. We must be willing to do the inner work before we try to call out the specks in others (Matthew 7:3–5). Healing is humbling, but it's also cleansing. And the truth is, these private moments of purification are the training ground. Because when the stage grows larger and your character is on display—without guardrails or training wheels—what will the audience see?

The spotlight will only expose what the secret place hasn't healed.

And finally, freedom requires maintenance. Paul understood this when he wrote, "I discipline my body and keep it under control, lest after preaching to others I myself should be disqualified" (1 Corinthians 9:27). Initial breakthrough must be followed by freedom-sustaining rhythms.

Spiritual builders who neglect this maintenance eventually experience influence regression. This convicting reality appears repeatedly—leaders who achieve significant impact but neglect ongoing inner work eventually collapse under unaddressed issues. If you won't heal it in private, it will haunt you in public.

Researcher and *Good to Great* author Jim Collins calls this "the undisciplined pursuit of more"—when people stretch too far, too fast, and lose what made them effective in the first place. Kingdom builders face a similar temptation to expand influence without expanding the internal freedom that sustains it.

In practical terms, freedom maintenance might include regular recalibration through retreats and extended prayer, honest accountability with trusted spiritual companions, and ongoing engagement with healing spaces like therapy, deliverance, or soul care. It also means honoring healthy boundaries even as demands increase and practicing ongoing forgiveness instead of silently collecting quiet offenses. These rhythms don't just preserve your soul, they protect your stewardship.

A FINAL WORD ON STAYING FREE

I know what it costs if I don't maintain freedom. I was there, walking with the Lord, anointed and discerning, yet still needing deeper healing to see people clearly and love without the filter of pain. I also had to confront my rescuer tendencies: trying to carry people who were resisting their next realm. The truth? I'm not called to rescue those stuck in resistance. I'm called to midwife those who are ready to reign, those emerging from storms, valleys, and wilderness seasons, hungry for purpose and aligned for breakthrough. That's where my oil flows. That's where legacy builds.

Senior Pastor of Bethel Church in Redding, California, Pastor Bill Johnson, wisely notes: "I can only lead people where I've gone myself." This principle applies to freedom territories—you effectively guide others only through liberation landscapes you've personally navigated. Your commitment to ongoing freedom work directly determines your long-term Kingdom impact.

SACRED EXERCISE

In what specific areas has God already brought freedom that's strengthening your ability to build? Where do you sense the Holy Spirit prompting you to pursue ongoing freedom to sustain your current influence or prepare for the next level of impact? How could consistent attention to these areas position you—and what you're building—for greater fruitfulness over the next five years?

CHAPTER 48

BECOMING A HEALED BUILDER: YOUR COMMISSIONING

Divine, as we prepare to close this vital chapter on healing before building, hear Heaven's invitation resounding through the ages: Broken vessels repaired by the Master's hand carry living water most powerfully. Your wounds, fully healed, become portals of divine presence for others. Your scars, touched by resurrection, become evidence of supernatural restoration.

The Father is not merely patching you up to function, He is fundamentally reconstructing you to flourish. This deep healing work prepares you for sustainable Kingdom-building—not just momentary ministry, but multigenerational impact. You are being formed as a cornerstone, not just a stepping stone.

I remember being invited to speak at the annual Disney Dreamers Academy—a vibrant, high-profile event filled with celebrities and cultural icons like Steve Harvey, Yolanda Adams, Raven-Symoné, and Terrence J, alongside media executives from Essence and other major outlets. I was there to lead a branding training, but what the

Spirit revealed had little to do with platforms and everything to do with purpose.

Before I even boarded the plane—and again after I arrived—I kept having a recurring vision. I saw hundreds of thousands of faceless women bowed low at the base of a stage, hands lifted in deep worship and travail. I stood on that stage, sister-friends of great influence—women of faith, power, and public prominence—positioned behind me on risers. I turned to them and said, "We've got to go to them." Without hesitation, they replied, "Let's go." And each time, the vision ended with our hands reaching down to link with the women below.

I didn't fully understand it at the time, so I asked a few trusted, Spirit-led sisters who were at Disney with me. Their insights confirmed what the Lord revealed weeks later: The women I saw represented those who would be impacted by my own healing journey. My authenticity and emotional freedom weren't just for me, they would become the very permission, courage, and boldness other women needed to rise and be healed. That vision was a prophetic picture of my mantle: to reach for women bowed in brokenness and midwife their rise into boldness, wholeness, and Kingdom identity.

Understand this profound truth: Every healing touch you receive becomes healing capacity you carry. The specific wounds God has healed in your life directly correspond to the specific restoration you'll bring to others. Your rejection healing enables you to create genuine belonging. Your trauma recovery equips you to establish authentic safety. Your voice restoration empowers you to commission silenced voices.

This is your inheritance as a healed builder—constructing from wholeness rather than woundedness. Not perfect, but progressively transformed. Not flawless, but fundamentally free. Not without weakness, but without debilitating brokenness that distorts what you build.

And while that vision pointed to what was coming, I had already begun to witness the power of healing in the rooms I was called to.

In the years leading up to that moment, my work often placed me in private spaces with prominent voices in the faith community—international televangelists, gospel artists, Christian actresses, and seasoned men in ministry from apostles to bishops. Whether they led a close-knit flock or pastored multiple campuses, even flying by helicopter between services, God would allow me to see them— *truly see them*—beyond the platform polish. I could often discern deep, unhealed places still affecting their peace, their leadership, and their ability to fully walk in breakthrough. Time and time again, I was led to gently reveal the connection between their healing, their hidden hurt, and the higher assignments waiting on the other side of wholeness for them and the people they were called to lead.

The time has come to fully commit to building from healed identity rather than compensating for hidden wounds. The structures you establish will only be as healthy as you are. Choose, therefore, the sometimes painful path of thorough healing before expansive building. The Kingdom cannot continue to afford wounded warriors constructing crooked towers.

....

"I have to surround myself with the right people to advise me. I GLADLY call Tia my mentor!" In fact, just from our 1-on-1 initial phone conversation she gave me a strategy that I implemented in my church immediately. Just 48 hours later I saw an unheard of 300% increase in my mid-week healing service. Tia's gifting is indescribable!"

—Hart Ramsey, Pastor, Songwriter & Author

....

SACRED EXERCISE

Looking at the next three to six months of your building journey, identify:

1. What specific healing work needs prioritizing before your next level of influence?

2. Which relationships consistently nurture your healing and which drain your wholeness?

3. How can you intentionally structure your leadership to flow from healed identity rather than performance, people-

pleasing, or past wounds?

4. What would you build differently if you were operating from complete freedom rather than partial healing?

5. How will you recognize and celebrate healing progress rather than only measuring external building achievements?

SACRED PRAYER | *Beloved Builder, receive this commissioning as you prepare to construct from wholeness rather than woundedness:*

Father of restoration, I thank You for this Divine daughter whom You are healing deeply for Kingdom purpose. I declare over her life that every wound the enemy intended for destruction is being transformed into a wellspring of authority and anointing.

I break agreement with the lie that she must build while bleeding. I release her from the false burden of proving her worth through premature production. I silence every accusation that healing focus is selfish or unproductive.

Lord Jesus, just as You perfectly modeled character preparation before public ministry, I pray she would embrace divine timing—receiving full healing before full deployment. May she trust the hidden seasons as essential to sustainable impact.

Holy Spirit, continue Your meticulous restoration work in her innermost being. Heal rejection at root levels. Restore voice with uncompromised authority. Break generational building patterns that reproduce dysfunction. Release authentic identity that builds from divine DNA rather than human expectation.

I commission her as a healed builder who constructs shelters of grace rather than structures of striving. May what she builds reflect wholeness, not compensate for woundedness. May her leadership create space for others' healing because she has walked the journey herself.

Lord, strengthen her resolved commitment to ongoing freedom maintenance. Even as influence expands, keep her humble enough to continue healing work. Make her a model of sustained inner liberty that produces sustained outer legacy.

I declare she is moving from healed to whole to commissioned—ready for the mantle of expanded influence that awaits in the next chapter.

In the mighty name of Jesus, our Healer and Builder, Amen.

Crowned for Influence

CHAPTER 49

CROWNED, NOT CASTED

You didn't audition for this. You were chosen.

The weight you carry—the voice, the vision, the spiritual intelligence, the influence—it didn't come by chance or human selection. It's a divine coronation. You are crowned, not casted.

This distinction is critical. We live in a world obsessed with visibility. Platforms are pursued as if the role goes to the most impressive résumé. But your influence is not a role you won, it's a calling you received.

Many women have been carrying a crown without even knowing it. You've been navigating visibility wounds—wrestling with the tension between being seen and being safe. One part of you longs to step fully into the light of purpose; another part fears the spotlight because you've been burned, or because you thought humility meant hiding.

But here's Heaven's gentle thunder: You were born for visibility—not vanity, but visibility that is sacred and set apart. You were selected—not scouted by an agent, but chosen by God before time—to stand out, to stand up, and to stand in the gap.

This takes me back to one of the first times I was publicly commissioned to obey the Holy Spirit's nudges in unfamiliar arenas. My husband and I were serving with our dear friends Bishop Kevin LeVar and his wife Shondale during a major ministry launch in Washington. No matter where we were, late-night prayer was always non-negotiable.

That night, Kevin released a prophetic word over us, and what he said to me was both exciting and weighty. The Lord was releasing fresh downloads and revelation for new arenas I would be sent into. But then came the warning: "The stages will get bigger, but you must say exactly what God gives you. If not, shame will follow and the people won't respect the gift." That word shook me. He anointed my ears right there in the room.

Less than a month later, I found myself flying to the West Coast with a colleague for a private meeting with celebrity father Matthew Knowles. After a tour of Destiny's Child's original studio and award room, I sat in his office, hoping to observe quietly. But the Holy Spirit reminded me, and Kevin's word stirred in my spirit. I opened my mouth and delivered exactly what God gave me. His response stunned the entire room. All I'll say is: God got the glory.

But it didn't stop there.

Days later, I was set to host red carpet interviews and teach branding at Dr. Holly Carter's amazingly anointed annual Merge Conference in LA. Imagine Black Hollywood royalty—Denzel Washington, Morris Chestnut, Boris Kodjoe, and many more—all gathered for faith-infused influence. During my session, I was on panel with executives from BET and NBC Universal when I said aloud, "Stop waiting to be casted when you're already called. Stop showing up like cattle hoping to be chosen—you are the opportunity."

There was a media exec there who tried to cut my mic. I was honestly relieved because I was nervous. And wouldn't you know, my ministry buddy/prophet Kevin happened to be standing in the back of the room. So not a coincidence.

But the crowd wasn't having it. They pushed back: "Let her speak." And I did—every word God gave me.

I missed the green room mixer afterward because a line formed. People waited to be prayed for, to tell their story, to be seen. It went on so long security had to escort me out through a back alley.

You can't make this up.

That's the weight of this moment we're in.

Indeed, modern prophetic voices affirm that we are in a season where God is strategically elevating His people into positions of influence across society. Many who were hidden in preparation will now be thrust forward by God's hand—not for personal glory, but to fulfill divine assignments in key spheres.

It's a fulfillment of what Isaiah 60 declares: "Nations and kings will come to the brightness of God's rising people."

So if you feel God drawing you into greater visibility, know this: Your rise is part of a larger move of God in this generation—Heaven placing its daughters where their Kingdom impact is needed most.

This is what it means to be crowned for influence. It means what you carry is not just a gift—it's a governance. You've been entrusted with something that carries authority, whether in prayer closets or boardrooms.

Now is the time to wear that mantle openly—for God's glory and others' good.

THE ANATOMY OF A DIVINE CORONATION

Let's pause to understand what it means when Heaven crowns you. This isn't a metaphor, it's a spiritual transaction with tangible impact. In Scripture, crowns consistently symbolize divine authorization, covenant, inheritance, and victory. When Samuel anointed David, for example, it wasn't a ceremonial gesture, it marked Heaven's official authorization for him to operate in a specific domain of leadership (1 Samuel 16:13). In Ezekiel 16:12, God places a crown on Jerusalem as an expression of covenant: "I put a ring on your nose, earrings on your ears and a beautiful crown on your head." Your crown is tethered to relationship. It signifies God's commitment to cover, guide, and back you as you step into visibility.

Crowns also signify inheritance. Proverbs 27:24 implies that crowns are not guaranteed to last across generations, they must be stewarded intentionally. What God places on you isn't for prestige alone, it's meant to bless others and build legacy. And finally, your crown points to victory. In 2 Timothy 4:8, Paul speaks of the "crown of righteousness" awaiting those who finish their race. That kind of crowning doesn't just represent achievement, it signifies that something has already been settled in the spirit.

Unlike worldly fame or promotion, divine coronation comes with a weight of glory—what the Apostle Paul called "an eternal weight of glory beyond all comparison" (2 Corinthians 4:17). It's not a burden that breaks you; it's a mantle that anchors you. This weight grounds your identity, fortifies your character, and lends substance to your presence. People will often sense it before you speak: "This one carries something of Heaven."

But with crown comes cross. Jesus modeled this perfectly. His coronation came not through celebration, but crucifixion. And yours may cost you comfort, convenience, or even relationships. The real question isn't whether you're ready to be seen. It's whether you're ready to surrender.

SACRED EXERCISE

What area of influence do you sense God specifically crowning you for in this season? What evidence do you have that this is divine appointment rather than personal ambition?

Now, find a quiet place and ask the Holy Spirit to reveal any "visibility wounds" that have caused you to hide your crown. Renounce any agreements with fear of being seen or the belief that humility means invisibility.Declare: "I receive my divine coronation. I accept the authority and responsibility that comes with it."

CHAPTER 50

ANOINTED TO BE SEEN

You are not arrogant for being visible.
You are anointed for it.

Somewhere along the journey of faith, many women of God were taught to fear the spotlight. We were warned, "Don't show off. Don't chase fame. It's not about you." Those warnings, meant to guard against pride, sometimes translated into an unintended commandment: "Thou shalt hide." So we learned to shrink. To stay behind the scenes. To defer, downplay, and delay.

We became masters of hiding. We spiritualized invisibility and called it maturity. We confused meekness with mousiness. All while a world in darkness was desperate to see the light we carry. The enemy revels in these misapplications of humility because if he can keep the daughters of the King in the shadows, he effectively silences a major threat.

Beloved, hear this clearly: God did not anoint you to stay hidden forever. Hiddenness is a season, not a lifestyle. Like seeds, we all start buried in the soil of God's preparation, but eventually He intends us to sprout. Jesus said, "No one lights a lamp and puts it under a bowl. Instead, they put it on a stand, and it gives light to everyone ..." (Matthew 5:15). You are that lamp lit by the fire of God. To hide you would be to waste divine fire.

Anointing is not just personal, it is public. "The Spirit of the Lord is upon Me, because He has anointed Me to proclaim good news to the poor ..." Jesus read in Luke 4:18. See the pattern? The Spirit anointed Him to proclaim. There was a vocal, visible assignment attached. Visibility was part of the obedience. So why do so many of us wrestle with fear of being seen?

The answer often lies in visibility wounds. Perhaps you were exposed prematurely and got hurt. Perhaps you saw someone mishandle fame and vowed, "I'll never become like that." Maybe you equated virtue with staying low-profile. But God is healing those wounds now. He's retraining our perspective—when He raises you up, it's safe. Being seen in His timing and way is secure, because you're shielded by His glory.

Yes, being visible for Christ will attract critics (it did for Jesus, Paul, and many others). But it will also attract those who are destined to connect with your calling. You become a city on a hill (Matthew 5:14), a beacon for the broken to find hope.

So come out of hiding. It's time. Being overly concerned with not appearing prideful can ironically become pride—an over-focus on self (even if negative). Shift your focus to Jesus and the people He loves. You'll find courage to step up when you realize it's not about *you* looking good; it's about God looking good to those who need Him.

THE WILDERNESS BEFORE THE PALACE

Before your public coronation comes private preparation. This pattern is consistent throughout Scripture — the calling happens early, but the crowning comes after character is forged.

Why? Because influence without integrity will eventually implode. Take King Saul, who began with humility, hiding among the baggage when called to be king (1 Samuel 10:22). Yet without proper heart preparation, his crown became his downfall. The very position meant to bless Israel became Saul's idol. He grew jealous, paranoid, and controlling—his crown becoming a curse.

Or consider Solomon, crowned with unparalleled wisdom and wealth. At first, he built the temple and ruled with justice. But without maintaining intimacy with God, his crown grew heavy, his heart divided, his focus diluted by foreign women and their gods (1 Kings 11:4).

This is why your wilderness season was not wasted time. In those lonely, unseen years, God was building in you what would sustain you when the crown came:

- Intimacy with Him that anchors you when visibility grows and applause surrounds
- Identity in Him that steadies you when critics rise and opinions swirl

- Integrity before Him that ensures your influence remains rooted and real
- Insight from Him that guides your decisions with wisdom beyond the spotlight

Think about Joseph's thirteen years between his dream and his promotion to Egypt's leadership. In prison, he developed the character that would later sustain his crown. When he finally stood before Pharaoh, Joseph didn't clamor for recognition, he pointed to God's interpretation (Genesis 41:16). His crown didn't change his character, it revealed it.

So if you've been in a prolonged wilderness, not seeing the fulfillment of prophetic words about your influence, take heart. The King is preparing you so thoroughly because He intends to trust you with so much. Your preparation is proportional to your promotion. Your hiddenness has been Heaven's protection until you were ready to bear the weight of the crown without it crushing you.

SACRED EXERCISE

How did your wilderness seasons prepare you for the crown you're now receiving? What character qualities were developed in hiddenness that will sustain you in visibility?

Take inventory of any areas where you still feel unprepared for greater influence. Bring these before the Lord in prayer:

"Father, continue to strengthen me in these areas. I want to steward well what You entrust to me." Listen for His response and guidance.

CHAPTER 51

ROYAL DECREES: WHY YOUR VOICE IS STRATEGIC

Your voice is not decoration. It is dominion.

In the Kingdom of God, words are not filler, they are formation. From the very beginning, God created by speaking. "Let there be ..." and it was. As His image-bearers—especially as Divine daughters— our words carry creative and authoritative power. Life and death are in the power of the tongue (Proverbs 18:21).

This is why the enemy has been after your voice from the start. He doesn't just fear your potential, he fears your proclamation. Because when a woman of God declares the Word of God into the atmosphere, things shift. Chains break. Angels move. Demons flee. This is not hyperbole, this is spiritual reality.

Believers have the authority to "shift atmospheres" through their prayers and decrees. When you speak God's truth into a room, the spiritual climate changes. Darkness must retreat as light floods in. You've likely experienced this—walking into a tense meeting and quietly binding strife, or entering a fearful situation and speaking peace, and the atmosphere literally becomes lighter. That's the power of a Spirit-anointed voice. Spiritual warfare isn't always loud or dramatic; it's frequently the steady, faith-filled declaration of God's Word that pushes back the enemy's influence. Never underestimate the authority God has given your voice. When you open your mouth in alignment with Heaven, you enforce Jesus' victory in the environment around you.

That, beloved, is spiritual warfare. It's not always casting out demons dramatically (though it can be). It's often the faithful, bold speaking of truth where it's needed. The enemy tries to shut up truth by intimidation or deception. But not on our watch. "She opens her mouth with wisdom, and the teaching of kindness is on her tongue" (Proverbs 31:26). Wisdom and kindness—what a combination—flow when you open your mouth under the Spirit's anointing. This world has enough noise; it needs anointed voices.

Your voice is not just sound, it is strategy. That's why hell tried to silence it early through shame ("be quiet"), trauma ("you have nothing of value to say"), false doctrine ("women should never speak"), or plain old fear. Satan knew your voice would be a key weapon, so he tried to dull or distort it. But God is giving it back to you now, refined and roaring.

Think of Deborah. She didn't raise her voice for popularity, she raised it because Israel needed direction. When she sang her victory song, she noted that village life revived "when I, Deborah, arose, arose a mother in Israel" (Judges 5:7). When she took her place and used her voice, life returned.

Think of Esther. At first, she was quiet, blending in. But when the stakes became clear, she found her voice—"If I perish, I perish"—and she pleaded for her people (Esther 4:16). Her voice saved a nation from genocide.

God is awakening the Deborahs and Esthers of this era. Deborah's bold leadership and Esther's courageous intercession are not just history, they are mantles available now. You carry a measure of these same anointings. When you speak up with Deborah's righteous authority, strongholds break. When you step out with Esther's bravery and sacrifice, deliverance comes to many. Heaven has called you, like Deborah, to be a mother in your sphere, and like Esther, to use royal position for Kingdom cause. You have a voice like theirs—use it.

Even Mary, the mother of Jesus, made a decree when she said, "Be it unto me according to Your word" (Luke 1:38). Her "yes" echoed through eternity and the Word became flesh in her womb.

Each of these women unlocked destiny with their words. And you will too.

THE AUTHORITY OF
HEAVEN-ALIGNED WORDS

When your words align with Heaven's agenda, they carry Heaven's authority. This is what Jesus meant when He said, "I tell you the truth, whatever you bind on earth will be bound in heaven, and whatever you loose on earth will be loosed in heaven" (Matthew

18:18). Your declarations, when in alignment with God's heart and timing, release or restrict spiritual realities.

Consider how Jesus operated: He constantly spoke what He heard the Father saying (John 12:49). His words weren't random, they were revelatory. They were strategic. When He told the storm "Peace, be still," nature had to obey because His word carried divine authority (Mark 4:39).

You've been given similar authority in your sphere. This isn't presumption, it's your inheritance as a daughter of the King. When you speak into your home, your workplace, your ministry field, your city, those words carry creative and transformative power.

But here's the key: This authority is relational, not mechanical. It doesn't work like a magic formula. It flows from intimacy with God. The more attuned you are to His heart, the more your words will carry His weight. This is why prayer (listening) must precede proclamation (speaking). You first hear in the secret place what you then declare in the public place.

So how do you wield this? Through royal decrees—authoritative statements aligned with God's will. They are not presumptuous demands, they are faith-filled declarations that release God's power.

Start in private. Speak Scripture over your life, family, city. For example, "I decree that no weapon formed against my household will prosper. I declare my children (or spiritual children) will serve the Lord. I announce that where I work, I carry the favor and presence of God, and darkness must flee." It might feel awkward at first, but you're training to use your sword.

Then in public, use your voice for God's glory. Share your testimony when prompted, articulate Kingdom values in meetings, encourage the discouraged, rebuke injustice, comfort the afflicted. Don't hold back the words of life bubbling inside. "The mouth of the righteous is a fountain of life" (Proverbs 10:11).

Remember, your voice has a jurisdiction. There are people only your voice will reach effectively. There are assignments attached to your voiceprint. That's why comparisons to others are futile. If you don't speak, something God wanted to say might go unheard because it was your assignment to say it.

But here's the beautiful synergy: As you use your voice, others will find theirs. Your boldness will spark boldness in them. This is part of your legacy—a chorus of liberated voices speaking because you dared to speak.

So, what will you decree in this season? Write down a few "I declare..." statements that align with Scripture and the vision God gave you. Speak them daily. Heaven is listening, and Heaven moves at the sound of God's Word on the lips of faith.

SACRED EXERCISE

What areas in your life, relationships, or mission need the power of your authoritative voice? Draft three to five scriptural declarations to speak over these areas.

Find a place where you can speak aloud. Choose one of your

declarations and speak it with authority. Pay attention to any resistance you feel—this often indicates where the enemy has tried to silence you. Push through that resistance with an even stronger declaration.

CHAPTER 52

KINGDOM INFLUENCE VS. WORLDLY AMBITION

Not all influence is created equal. One springs from Heaven's purpose, the other from human pride. As you step into your crown, you must discern the critical difference between Kingdom influence and worldly ambition. The outcomes couldn't be more different.

Kingdom influence builds God's legacy, while worldly ambition builds personal platforms. One serves, the other showcases. One is motivated by love, the other by recognition. Learning to distinguish between the two will preserve both your ministry and your soul.

PLATFORM IDOLATRY: THE MODERN GOLDEN CALF

In ancient Israel, while Moses received God's commandments on the mountain, the people grew impatient and built a golden calf to worship (Exodus 32). Today, we face a similar temptation with different materials. Our golden calf isn't made of precious metal, but of precious metrics—followers, likes, speaking invitations, book deals, conference stages.

Platform idolatry happens when legitimate ministry tools become illegitimate objects of trust. When influence morphs from a means of serving to a means of self-validation. When numbers become the measure of your worth rather than your faithfulness.

But how did this modern golden calf take shape in the first place?

Drawing from my graduate studies in brand communications, I understand how this evolution unfolded. In the early 1900s—what we now call the industrial era—it was all about mass production: widgets, gadgets, and early inventions. By the 1960s, we entered the consumer era. Brands began to realize it wasn't just about the product, it was about the people buying it. Slowly, they started listening to the voice of the consumer.

Then came the early 2000s and the relational era, fueled by the rise of reality television and social media. This era didn't just change how we connect, it changed who we see as credible. Expertise took a back seat to relatability. And just like that, the age of the influencer was born.

Now, being an influencer in itself isn't wrong, but it absolutely matters who you're being influenced by. Are you reflecting the heart of the King, or being swayed by the pull of culture, comparison, and clout?

If you carry influence in this season, it's worth paying attention to the subtle signs that your platform may be turning into a golden calf. You may notice rising anxiety when engagement metrics dip, or envy creeping in when others' platforms grow faster. Your decisions may begin to revolve around visibility rather than obedience. If your ministry identity starts hinging on public recognition—or if you find yourself restless or discontent when your service goes unseen—these are gentle alarms from the Spirit. They aren't meant to shame, but to shepherd your heart back into alignment.

Jesus directly addressed this heart condition: "Be careful not to practice your righteousness in front of others to be seen by them. If you do, you will have no reward from your Father in heaven" (Matthew 6:1). The warning is clear: when recognition becomes your reward, you forfeit Heaven's deeper blessing.

Think about it. Jesus had every opportunity to build a massive platform. He could have stationed Himself in Jerusalem, performed daily miracles, and amassed millions of followers. Instead, He often withdrew from crowds, told the healed not to publicize their miracles, and invested deeply in just twelve. His approach to influence was kingdom-focused, not crowd-focused.

This doesn't mean visibility is wrong. But your heart's posture in visibility makes all the difference. When you're more concerned with faithfulness than followers, more devoted to pleasing God than impressing people, you're protected from platform idolatry.

TESTING THE MOTIVES
BEHIND YOUR INFLUENCE

How do you know if your influence is Kingdom-oriented or self-serving? Here are some diagnostic questions:

1. Would you continue in your calling if no one ever recognized your work?

2. Do you feel genuine joy when others in your field gain visibility and success?

3. Can you honestly say before God that your primary motivation is love for Him and others, not recognition?

4. Are you willing to do things that diminish your platform but advance God's Kingdom?

5. Does your peace depend more on God's approval than public acclaim?

This is why, in earlier chapters, we focused heavily on our inner man over our public profile. We have to stay in step with the Holy Spirit. And I'm not omitted. This reminds me to make sure I've got my SEO days locked in with my Sovereign Executive Officer. Without Father, Son and Holy Ghost, I don't like my own heart.

These aren't questions to condemn but to clarify. All of us battle mixed motives. The key is regularly bringing our ambitions before the Lord for refining and realignment.

Consider King David's heart-check prayer: "Search me, God, and know my heart; test me and know my anxious thoughts. See if there is any offensive way in me, and lead me in the way everlasting" (Psalm 139:23-24). This is a prayer of a leader determined to maintain pure motives.

By contrast, true Kingdom influence bears unmistakable marks. It always points to Jesus, not self. Like John the Baptist, its quiet posture is: "He must increase, but I must decrease" (John 3:30). It gives without strings, asking not "What will I gain?" but "How can I serve?" It remains steady in obscurity, showing up with the same passion whether ten or ten thousand are watching. It celebrates others without competition, finding joy in their rise because it values Kingdom advancement above personal advancement. And it measures impact by lives transformed, not platforms expanded. Numbers don't impress the Spirit—obedience does.

When your influence flows from these values, you become truly dangerous to darkness, because you cannot be manipulated by the promise of recognition or the threat of obscurity. Your crown sits securely on your head because it's not dependent on human approval but on divine appointment.

SACRED EXERCISE

What aspects of platform or recognition have you been tempted to idolize? How would your ministry change if no one but God knew what you were doing?

Take a social media fast for three to seven days. During this time, ask God to reveal any areas where platform has become an idol. Listen for His affirmation of your true identity apart from public validation.

CHAPTER 53

SIGNS OF A DIVINE CROWNING SEASON

My goal is to ensure that Esthers don't abort their authority simply because they didn't realize they were royalty. Remember, Mordecai had to snap Esther out of her hesitation. He told her plainly, "If you remain silent at this time, relief and deliverance ... will arise from another place" (Esther 4:14). In other words, "Sis, if you don't move now, you might miss your crowning moment."

I always say momentum is not obligated to do a personal encore. As beautiful, poised, and gifted as you may be, it's not a good look to be chasing a caboose. Once that train leaves the station, that door closes, that moment shifts, that window of divine timing passes. Some opportunities don't circle back. That's why you must discern the signs of your divine crowning season.

So how do you know when you're entering a season of increased influence? There are spiritual signals that often accompany it. You may face heightened opposition—the kind that suggests hell has taken notice because Heaven is advancing you. Unusual resistance often confirms you're on the edge of breakthrough.

At the same time, you may begin to witness doors opening that you didn't knock on. Opportunities arrive unprompted. Divine connections begin forming without your orchestration—clear evidence that Heaven is positioning you.

Others may begin speaking confirming prophetic words over your life, often with surprising detail about your call and reach—things you haven't publicly disclosed. These affirmations come not to inflate, but to affirm what Heaven has already been stirring.

That stirring will likely rise internally as well. A holy restlessness may begin to grow, a prompting that it's time to increase your voice and expand your territory. This isn't about ambition, it's about assignment.

Your heart may also start to break for people and issues outside your usual circles. Instead of just thinking about individuals, you'll begin thinking about systems. This is a sign your influence is maturing beyond personal preference and into societal burden.

And don't be surprised if your growth accelerates. What once took you years to grasp may take months. Heaven speeds up your development when the urgency of your assignment demands it.

If you're experiencing these signs, rejoice! But also prepare. Greater influence brings greater spiritual warfare, greater scrutiny, and greater need for character strength. This is why intimate communion with God becomes even more critical as your crown becomes more visible.

GUARDING THE CROWN
YOU'VE BEEN ENTRUSTED WITH

Power tests character like nothing else. I've reported too many stories to count—both in newsrooms and in ministry—where influence exposed what discipline failed to address. That's why your crown must be protected with intentional guardrails. Accountability must deepen as your platform expands. Make room for wise voices who can ask the hard questions and keep your soul anchored. Transparency is another safeguard—secrecy only breeds corruption in the dark. Choose to live openly before God and trusted counsel.

Humility is your protection against pride. Serve in hidden places and welcome feedback that keeps your ego in check. Set clear ethical boundaries in areas like finances, relationships, and decision-making. Write them down and share them with your people or sacred team. Most of all, never forget that your influence is a stewardship, not a right. It belongs to God, not to you. What you've received is on loan. And that's why intimacy with Him must come before the activity done for Him. As demands increase, so must your commitment to the secret place. Elijah, after calling down fire, didn't run to another revival, he collapsed under a broom tree, then met God in the whisper (1 Kings 19). That's where true crowns are recalibrated—not on stages, but in surrender.

Your crown is most vulnerable when you begin to believe it's yours by merit rather than by mercy. When King Uzziah achieved great things, his heart became proud, and he entered the temple to burn incense—a task reserved for priests. His unauthorized action resulted in leprosy (2 Chronicles 26:16-20). It's a harsh reminder that even godly success can lead to presumption if we forget our boundaries and responsibilities.

The antidote to the corruption of power is your consistent surrender. Each morning, place your crown back at Jesus' feet and ask for the grace to wear it humbly and effectively that day. This daily surrender keeps your heart tender and your leadership trustworthy.

SACRED EXERCISE

What specific temptations or pressures do you anticipate as your influence grows? What safeguards will you put in place to protect your heart and integrity?

Write a personal "Crown Covenant"—a commitment between you and God regarding how you'll steward influence. Include your boundaries, accountability structure, and regular practices that will keep you grounded in humility.

CHAPTER 54

SACRED IDENTITY LEADING TO SACRED INFLUENCE

Throughout this book, we've emphasized a critical progression: **Sacred Identity must precede Sacred Influence**. Your being comes before your building. Who you are in Christ establishes what you'll accomplish for Christ. When I worked with clients in the past, they'd say, "I want to be positioned this way or branded that way." I'd say, "Working with me is about positioning God's way."

This sequence is non-negotiable because influence without identity becomes toxic both to you and to those you lead. When you don't know who you are, you'll use others to define you. When you're unclear about your worth, you'll use work to prove it. But when identity is secure, influence can flow purely without the contamination of ego or insecurity.

Look at Moses. Before God sent him to influence a nation, He established Moses' identity: "I AM has sent you" (Exodus 3:14). Moses wasn't representing himself, he was representing I AM. His influence was an extension of his connection to God.

The same is true for you. Your crown doesn't define you, it express-es who you already are in Christ. This is why all the identity work in earlier chapters wasn't preliminary, it was foundational. You can't give what you don't have. You can't lead where you haven't been. You can't release what you haven't received.

Consider how this divine sequence unfolded in the life of Priscilla Shirer. As she has often shared in interviews and teachings, long before her name became widely known through books, films, or global conferences, she was a seminary student, faithfully study-ing God's Word and serving quietly under her father's leadership at church. Her public influence came only after years of deep iden-tity work in private. Even today, she consistently reminds audienc-es that her highest identity isn't as a speaker or author, but as a daughter of the King. Her authority flows not from platform polish but from spiritual rootedness. Her story reminds us—identity first, then influence.

When this divine order is truly understood, everything shifts. You stop striving, because you realize your value isn't in what you build but in who you are. This breaks performance addiction. You begin abiding more than performing, prioritizing connection with God over accomplishment for God. Your fruitfulness starts flowing out of fellowship. You start to seek impact, not importance. The goal becomes transformation of others, not admiration from others. And you begin to lead from overflow, not obligation. Ministry be-comes the natural expression of what God is doing in you, not a role you force yourself to fulfill.

Knowing that who you are in Christ matters infinitely more than what you accomplish for Christ is freeing. This freedom enables you to accomplish far more of eternal significance because you're no longer constrained by fear, comparison, or the need for validation.

So as you step into greater influence, remember: **Your crown doesn't make you royal**. You wear the crown because you are already royal—a daughter of the King. The external recognition is simply catching up to the internal reality.

REFLECTION AND CORONATION: FOR SUCH A TIME AS THIS

It was 1998, and Savannah State University's auditorium was packed. My peers, professors, family, supporters, and onlookers filled the room. The space had been transformed into a modern-day palace. Television trucks were stationed outside. A popular news anchor emceed the evening. And it was my coronation night.

I was being crowned Miss SSU.

I still remember the moment my beautiful mother walked gracefully across the stage and read a poem she had written just for me, her words echoing life and destiny into my soul. My queen's court was filled with hundreds of young women seated in position, regal and radiant.

And then it happened.

The president of the university placed the heavy blue cloak over my shoulders. My court of ladies placed the scepter in my hand. A ring on my finger. And the crown—yes, the crown—was set upon my head. As majestic as that experience was, that moment didn't make me royal, it revealed what Heaven already knew.

Selah.

If you've followed along and made it to this part of the book, I want you to pause with me and let this moment wash over you. Imagine the mantle, the scepter, and the crown being placed upon you right now.

Not just as a symbol. But as a confirmation.
Here you stand now, at the threshold of your own coronation.
Not an end. But a beginning.
Not a title. But a trust.

Like Esther dressing in royal robes to approach the king, like Deborah arising as a mother in Israel, you have come fully alive to who you are and what you carry.

This closing section is both reflection and activation, a holy pause to look back on how God has woven every chapter of your journey, and a bold step forward to bow—yes, bow—before the King as He places a crown of commission on your head.

RISE AND BE REVEALED

You've walked through the refining. You've received your crown. Now it's time to rise and be seen.

And if you're wondering … yes, this is your gentle nudge to start a Sacred Sister Circle. Nothing fancy. Just a gathering of women walking through these pages together or processing what God is awakening in their own lives. You can meet over coffee. Start a group text. Swap voice notes. Stream a chapter. Or simply reflect side-by-side with your best friend, journal in hand. Whether it's two or twenty, it matters. Let your Sacred Sister Circle be a space of anointed celebration, sisterhood, and strength.

And if you post or share your moment online, use the hashtag #DivineArise and tag me—I'd love to celebrate and shout you out.

FROM SACRED CIRCLE TO KINGDOM CALL

Before you move forward, take a few minutes to pause with the Lord and reflect:

- » What fears still linger about being seen or using your voice more boldly?

- » What boundaries will protect your intimacy with God as you rise?

- » What legacy are you building—not just now, but for three generations ahead?

Bonus: Write a letter from the Father's perspective to your future self. Let His voice affirm why He chose you for this crown.

When the moment feels right, download your Covenant of the Crown at www.divinearise.com, a printable declaration and prayer you can speak aloud, frame, or share with your Sacred Sister Circle.

If your heart is ready now, you can simply say: "God, I receive this crown not by merit, but by mercy. I commit to wear it with humility, wield it with love, and return it to You in full." Let that be your Amen.

You are no longer hidden. You are no longer questioning your worth. You are being revealed. You are not auditioning—you are already appointed. You are the evidence of Isaiah 60, but your journey will continue Psalm by Psalm—step by step. Let His Word remain your lamp and your light, even after the final page.

FINAL CHARGE: DIVINE, ARISE.

As you walk out this commissioned visibility, know that you carry more than influence—you carry inheritance.

So go—not to strive, but to govern. Not to be seen, but to reveal. Let your Kingdom allegiance show in how you love, lead, and lift others.

The evidence of your royalty won't be in how brightly you shine— but in how many others arise because you did.

Your legacy has already begun.

REFERENCES

Munroe, Myles. *Understanding the Purpose and Power of Women*. Whitaker House, 1992.

Dalton-Smith, Saundra. *Sacred Rest: Recover Your Life, Renew Your Energy, Restore Your Sanity*. FaithWords, 2017.

Phillips, Anita. Various online teachings and podcast interviews, 2020–2024.

Sumrall, Lester. *The Gifts and Ministries of the Holy Spirit*. Whitaker House, 2005.

Carter, Howard. *Questions and Answers on Spiritual Gifts*. Bridge-Logos, 1976.

Giles, Joshua. *When God Speaks*. Chosen Books, 2022.

Wright, Carl J. *God's Vision or Television*. Kingdom Business Publishers, 2009.

ABOUT THE AUTHOR

Tia Brewer-Footman is a prophetic leader, brand strategist, and former television anchor whose influence bridges faith, media, and the marketplace. A master communicator and founder of The Sacred Business Enterprise, she equips believers—especially women of faith—to discover their divine design and build sacred brands that impact culture.

With a career spanning representation, segmented event activations, and consulting for specialty initiatives with such global brands as Disney, McDonald's, Walmart, and dozens more, Tia brings over two decades of combined experience in media, leadership, and Kingdom strategy. An award-winning communicator and former anchor for ABC, CBS, and FOX affiliates, she reached more than 250,000 households daily before shifting her focus to equipping others to rise in their God-given callings.

Alongside her husband, Pastor Gerald Footman, she co-founded Footman-Brewer Enterprises, LLC and FootPrint Transit, LLC—ventures that merge excellence and ministry impact. Appointed by former South Carolina Governor Nikki Haley as a State Commissioner for Minority Affairs, Tia has also served on financial and civic boards for Truist Bank and other national community development initiatives.

A proud HBCU graduate and former Miss Savannah State University, she earned her master's degree in Brand Communication from Drake University. Her distinctions include Boeing's Women in Leadership Speaker, 40 Under 40, and "Tia Brewer Day" honors in both Charleston, South Carolina, and Buffalo, New York.

When she's not serving her community, stewarding brands, or supporting her husband in ministry, Tia enjoys spa days, quiet reflection, and relaxing on her back deck in the hot tub—her favorite way to unwind and simply be. She resides just outside of Charleston, South Carolina, where her life continues to reflect the beauty of balance between sacred purpose and personal peace.

www.ingramcontent.com/pod-product-compliance
Lightning Source LLC
Chambersburg PA
CBHW071625140626
46555CB00021B/58